This Art of Psychoanalysis

D1570280

This Art of Psychoanalysis offers a unique perspective on psychoanalysis that features a new way of conceptualizing the role of dreaming in human psychology.

Thomas Ogden's thinking has been at the cutting edge of psychoanalysis for more than 25 years. In this volume, he builds on the work of Freud, Klein, Winnicott, and Bion and explores the idea that human psychopathology is a manifestation of a breakdown of the individual's capacity to dream his experience. The investigation into the role of the analyst in participating psychologically in the patient's dreaming is illustrated throughout with elegant and absorbing accounts of clinical work, providing a fascinating insight into the analyst's experience. Subjects covered include:

- A new reading of the origins of object relations theory
- On holding and containing, being and dreaming
- On psychoanalytic writing

This engaging book succeeds in conveying not just a set of techniques but a way of being with patients that is humane and compassionate. It will be of great interest to psychoanalysts, psychotherapists and other mental health professionals.

Thomas H. Ogden is the winner of the *2004 International Journal of Psychoanalysis Award for Outstanding Paper*. He is the Director of the Centre for the Advanced Study of the Psychoses and a full member of the International Psychoanalytical Association.

THE NEW LIBRARY OF PSYCHOANALYSIS
General Editor Dana Birksted-Breen

The New Library of Psychoanalysis was launched in 1987 in association with the Institute of Psychoanalysis, London. It took over from the International Psychoanalytical Library which published many of the early translations of the works of Freud and the writings of most of the leading British and Continental psychoanalysts.

The purpose of the New Library of Psychoanalysis is to facilitate a greater and more widespread appreciation of psychoanalysis and to provide a forum for increasing mutual understanding between psychoanalysts and those working in other disciplines such as the social sciences, medicine, philosophy, history, linguistics, literature and the arts. It aims to represent different trends both in British psychoanalysis and in psychoanalysis generally. The New Library of Psychoanalysis is well placed to make available to the English-speaking world psychoanalytic writings from other European countries and to increase the interchange of ideas between British and American psychoanalysts.

The Institute, together with the British Psychoanalytical Society, runs a low-fee psychoanalytic clinic, organizes lectures and scientific events concerned with psychoanalysis and publishes the *International Journal of Psychoanalysis*. It also runs the only UK training course in psychoanalysis which leads to membership of the International Psychoanalytical Association – the body which preserves internationally agreed standards of training, of professional entry, and of professional ethics and practice for psychoanalysis as initiated and developed by Sigmund Freud. Distinguished members of the Institute have included Michael Balint, Wilfred Bion, Ronald Fairbairn, Anna Freud, Ernest Jones, Melanie Klein, John Rickman and Donald Winnicott.

Previous General Editors include David Tuckett, Elizabeth Spillius and Susan Budd. Previous and current Members of the Advisory Board include Christopher Bollas, Ronald Britton, Catalina Bronstein, Donald Campbell, Sara Flanders, Stephen Grosz, John Keene, Eglé Laufer, Juliet Mitchell, Michael Parsons, Rosine Jozef Perelberg, Richard Rusbridger, David Taylor and Mary Target.

ALSO IN THIS SERIES

TITLES IN THE NEW LIBRARY OF
PSYCHOANALYSIS TEACHING SERIES

THE NEW LIBRARY OF PSYCHOANALYSIS

General Editor: Dana Birksted-Breen

This Art of Psychoanalyis

Dreaming Undreamt Dreams and Interrupted Cries

Thomas H. Ogden

Routledge
Taylor & Francis Group

LONDON AND NEW YORK

First published 2005
by Routledge
27 Church Road, Hove, East Sussex, BN3 2FA

Simultaneously published in the USA and Canada
by Routledge
270 Madison Avenue, New York, NY 10016

Routledge is an imprint of the Taylor & Francis Group

Typeset in Bembo by Keystroke, Jacaranda Lodge, Wolverhampton
Printed and bound in Great Britain by
TJ International Ltd, Padstow, Cornwall
Paperback cover design by Sandra Heath

British Library Cataloguing in Publication Data
A catalogue record for this book is available from the British Library

Library of Congress Cataloging in Publication Data
Ogden, Thomas H.
This art of psychoanalysis : dreaming undreamt dreams and interrupted cries /
Thomas H. Ogden.
p. cm. — (New library of psychoanalysis)
Includes bibliographical references and index.
ISBN 0–415–37288–7 (hbk.) — ISBN 0–415–37289–5 (pbk.)
1. Psychoanalysis. 2. Dreams—Psychological aspects.
I. Title. II. New library of psychoanalysis (Unnumbered)
RC506.O345 2005
154.6′3—dc22
2005008605

ISBN 0–415–37288–7 (hbk)
ISBN 0–415–37289–5 (pbk)

With gratitude to the members, past and present,
of the Wednesday and Friday Seminars

Contents

Acknowledgments

Chapter 1 is based on "This art of psychoanalysis: dreaming undreamt dreams and interrupted cries," *International Journal of Psychoanalysis*, 85: 857–877, 2004. © Institute of Psychoanalysis, London, UK.

Chapter 3 is based on "A new reading of the origins of object-relations theory," *International Journal of Psychoanalysis*, 83: 767–782, 2002. © Institute of Psychoanalysis, London, UK.

Chapter 4 is based on "On not being able to dream," *International Journal of Psychoanalysis*, 84: 17–30, 2003. © Institute of Psychoanalysis, London, UK.

Chapter 5 is based on "What's true and whose idea was it?" *International Journal of Psychoanalysis*, 84: 593–606, 2003. © Institute of Psychoanalysis, London, UK.

Chapter 6 is based on "An introduction to the reading of Bion," *International Journal of Psychoanalysis*, 85: 285–300, 2004. © Institute of Psychoanalysis, London, UK.

Chapter 7 is based on "On holding and containing, being and dreaming," *International Journal of Psychoanalysis*, 85: 1349–1364, 2004. © Institute of Psychoanalysis, London, UK.

Chapter 8 is based on "On psychoanalytic writing," *International Journal of Psychoanalysis*, 86: 15–29, 2005. © Institute of Psychoanalysis, London, UK.

Excerpt from "I Could Give All to Time" from THE POETRY OF ROBERT FROST edited by Edward Connery Lathem. Copyright 1942 by Robert Frost, © 1970 by Lesley Frost Ballantine, © 1969 by Henry Holt and Company. Reprinted by permission of Henry Holt and Company, LLC. Published by Jonathan Cape. Reprinted by permssion of the Random House Group Ltd.

Excerpt from "Carpe Diem" from THE POETRY OF ROBERT FROST edited by Edward Connery Lathem. Copyright 1942, 1969 by Henry Holt and

Company, copyright 1938 by Robert Frost. Reprinted by permission of Henry Holt and Company, LLC. Published by Jonathan Cape. Reprinted by permssion of the Random House Group Ltd.

Excerpt from "Funes the Memorious" by Jorge Luis Borges, translated by James E. Irby, from LABYRINTHS, copyright ©1962, 1964 by New Directions Publishing Corp. Reprinted by permission of New Directions Publishing Corp.

Line from "Clearances, Sonnet III" from OPENED GROUND: SELECTED POEMS 1966–1996 by Seamus Heaney. Published by Farrar, Straus & Giroux, LLC, copyright 1999. Reprinted by permission.

Every effort has been made to trace copyright holders and obtain permission for quoted material. Any omissions brought to our attention will be remedied in future editions.

I am grateful to Marta Schneider Brody for her insightful comments on a number of drafts of the manuscript of this book and for creating the cover illustration. I would also like to thank Patricia Marra for the care and thought that she brought to preparing the manuscript of this volume for publication.

Preface

From the outset the writing of this book has had a highly personal feel to me. It has been an experience that has had something of the feel of writing a series of letters over a span of years to a colleague on the subject of how I am conceiving of psychoanalysis at this point in my life. I take fully for granted that all of what I currently believe regarding the theory and practice of psychoanalysis is in the process of changing even in the process of writing it (or, more accurately, particularly in the process of writing it). Borges (1970a) said that he spent his entire life re-writing his first book of published poems. I have a similar feeling with regard to my attempts to put into words my understanding of those aspects of psychoanalysis that are of most importance to me, and to say how they have become integral to who I am, and who I am becoming as a psychoanalyst. This book represents the most recent installment of that life-long effort.

This art of psychoanalysis: dreaming undreamt dreams and interrupted cries

I

It is the art of psychoanalysis in the making, a process inventing itself as it goes, that is the subject of this chapter. Psychoanalysis is a lived emotional experience. As such, it cannot be translated, transcribed, recorded, explained, understood or told in words. It is what it is. Nevertheless, I believe it is possible to say something about that lived experience that is of value in thinking about aspects of what it is that happens between analysts and their patients when they are engaged in the work of psychoanalysis.

I find it useful in my own thinking – which often occurs in the act of writing – to limit myself at first to using as few words as possible in an effort to capture essences of meaning. It is my experience that in psychoanalytic writing, as in poetry, a concentration of words and meaning draws on the power of language to suggest what it cannot say. In this chapter I begin by offering a highly condensed statement – the analytic process, as I conceive of it – and then go on to discuss more fully, that densely stated set of ideas. Since each element of my conception of psychoanalysis is inseparable from the others, there are many instances in this chapter where I double back on, or jump ahead of the initial sequential statement. (Perhaps this reflects something of the nature of the movement of the analytic experience itself.) I conclude by presenting a detailed account of an experience in which the patient and I were able to think, and speak, and dream (formerly) undreamt and interrupted dreams.

II

A person consults a psychoanalyst because he is in emotional pain, which unbeknownst to him, he is either unable to dream (i.e. unable to do unconscious psychological work) or is so disturbed by what he is dreaming that his dreaming is disrupted. To the extent that he is unable to dream his emotional experience, the individual is unable to change, or to grow, or to become anything other than who he has been. The patient and analyst engage in an experiment within the terms of the psychoanalytic situation that is designed to generate conditions in which the analysand (with the analyst's participation) may become better able to dream his undreamt and interrupted dreams. The dreams dreamt by the patient and analyst are at the same time their own dreams (and reveries) and those of a third subject who is both and neither patient and analyst.

In the course of participating in dreaming the patient's undreamt and interrupted dreams, the analyst gets to know the patient in a way and at a depth that may allow him to say something to the patient that is true to the conscious and unconscious emotional experience that is occurring in the analytic relationship at a given moment. What the analyst says must be utilizable by the patient for purposes of conscious and unconscious psychological work, i.e., for dreaming his own experience, thereby dreaming himself more fully into existence.[1]

III

Before I attempt to "unpack" the preceding statement, two sets of introductory comments are necessary: the first addresses the theoretical context for the discussion that follows; the second addresses a pair of metaphors for the psychic states in which patients come to analysis and with which they struggle during analysis.

An essential part of the theoretical background for the way I conceptualize the practice of psychoanalysis derives from (my interpretation of) Bion's theory of dreaming and of not being able to dream. (I have previously discussed this aspect of Bion's work [Ogden, 2003a] and will only very briefly summarize the relevant aspects of that discussion here.)

Bion (1962a) introduced the term "alpha-function" to refer to the as yet un-known set of mental functions which together transform raw "sense-impressions related to an emotional experience" (p.17), which he terms "beta-elements," into "alpha-elements." Beta-elements – unprocessed sense impressions – are unlinkable with one another and consequently cannot be utilized for thinking, dreaming or storage as memory. In contrast, alpha-elements are elements of experience that can be linked with one another in the process of conscious and unconscious thinking and dreaming (both while we are awake and asleep). For Bion,

> Failure of alpha-function means the patient cannot dream and therefore cannot sleep. [Inasmuch as] alpha-function makes the sense impressions of the emotional experience available for conscious [thought] and dream-thought, the patient who cannot dream cannot go to sleep and cannot wake

up. Hence the peculiar condition seen clinically when the psychotic patient behaves as if he were in precisely this state.

(1962a, pp. 6–7)

There are a number of thoughts here that are essential to the conception of psychoanalysis that I am presenting. Dreaming is an ongoing process occurring in both sleep and in unconscious waking life. If a person is incapable of transforming raw sense impressions into unconscious elements of experience that can be linked, he cannot generate unconscious dream-thoughts and consequently cannot dream (either in sleep or in unconscious waking life). The experience of raw sense impressions (beta-elements) in sleep is no different from the experience of beta-elements in waking life. Hence, the individual "cannot go to sleep and cannot wake up" (Bion, 1962a, p. 7), i.e. he cannot differentiate being asleep and being awake, perceiving and hallucinating, external reality and internal reality.

Conversely, not all psychic events occurring in sleep (even visual imagistic events) warrant the name *dream*. Psychological events occurring in sleep that resemble dreaming, but are not dreams, include "dreams" for which neither patient nor analyst is able to generate any associations, hallucinations in sleep, dreams consisting of a single imageless feeling state, the unchanging dreams of post-traumatic patients and (as will be discussed) night terrors. These "dreams" that are not dreams, involve no unconscious psychological work, nothing of the work of dreaming.

IV

The second of the two sets of comments that are required prior to considering my conception of doing psychoanalysis concerns the phenomena of nightmares and night terrors. I find that these two disturbances of sleep serve both as examples of, and metaphors for, two very broad categories of psychological functioning. Taken together, night terrors and nightmares, as I understand them, are emblematic of the stuff that the full range of human psychopathology is made of.

Nightmares are "bad dreams"; night terrors are "dreams" that are not dreams. Night terrors differ from nightmares not only in terms of phenomenology and psychological function, but also in terms of their neurophysiology and the brain wave activity associated with them.[2]

The child[3] having a night terror "awakens" in great fear, but does not recognize the parent who has been awakened by his cries and has come to comfort him. The child eventually calms and without discernible fear "returns to sleep." On "awakening" the next morning, the child has little or no recollection of the night terror or of having been comforted by his parent. In the rare event that a

3

child is able to remember anything at all of the night terror, it is a single image such as being chased or of "something sitting on me" (Hartmann, 1984, p. 18). The child does not evidence any fear in going to sleep the subsequent night. There is seemingly no conscious or unconscious memory of the experience. Both from a psychoanalytic point of view and from the point of view of brain wave activity, the person having a night terror does not wake up from the experience nor does he fall back to sleep after being calmed (Daws, 1989). A person having night terrors is unable to view them from the perspective of waking life. In Bion's terms, night terrors are constituted of raw sense impressions related to emotional experience (beta-elements), which cannot be linked in the process of dreaming, thinking or storage as memory. The child having night terrors can only genuinely wake up when he is able to dream his undreamt dream.

In contrast, a nightmare is an actual dream (which occurs in REM sleep) that "*awakens the person* with a scared feeling" (Hartmann, 1984, p. 10, emphasis added). On awakening, the dreamer is able immediately, or within a relatively short period of time, to differentiate between being awake and being asleep, perceiving and dreaming, internal reality and external reality. Consequently, the individual is often able to remember the manifest content of the nightmare on waking and able to think and talk about it. The child who has been awoken by a nightmare is able to recognize the person who is comforting him, and, because he can remember having had a nightmare, is afraid to go back to sleep that night, and commonly for weeks or months afterwards.

In sum, a nightmare is quite different from a night terror. The former is a dream in which the individual's emotional pain is subjected (to a significant degree) to unconscious psychological work that issues in psychological growth. However, that dreaming is disrupted at a point where the individual's capacity for generating dream-thoughts and dreaming them is overwhelmed by the disturbing effects of the emotional experience being dreamt. A night terror is not a dream; no dream-thoughts are generated; no psychological work is done; nothing changes as a consequence of the psychic event.

V

With Bion's conception of dreaming as a theoretical context and the phenomena of nightmares and night terrors as metaphors for two broad categories of psychological functioning, it is now possible to begin systematically to scrutinize the elements of the compact statement I made earlier regarding my conception of psychoanalysis.

To begin at the beginning: *A person consults a psychoanalyst because he is in emotional pain, which unbeknownst to him, he is either unable to dream (i.e., unable to do unconscious psychological work) or is so disturbed by what he is dreaming that his dreaming is disrupted. To the extent that he is unable to dream his emotional experience, the individual is unable to change, or to grow, or to become anything other than who he has been.*

Some patients who consult an analyst might be thought of as suffering from (metaphorical) night terrors. Without being aware of it, they are seeking help in dreaming their undreamt and undreamable experience. The undreamt dreams of such patients persist unchanged as split-off pockets (or broad sectors) of psychosis (Bion, 1962a) or as aspects of the personality in which experience is foreclosed from psychological elaboration. Among the disorders characterized by such foreclosure are the psychosomatic disorders and severe perversions (de M'Uzan, 1984); autistic encapsulation in bodily sensation (Tustin, 1981); "dis-affected" states (McDougall, 1984) in which patients are unable to "read" their emotions and bodily sensations; and the schizophrenic state of "non-experience" (Ogden, 1982) where the chronic schizophrenic patient attacks his own capacity for attributing meaning to experience thus rendering emotional experiences interchangeable with one another. In disorders involving psychic foreclosure, the patient's thinking is, to a very large degree, of an operational sort (de M'Uzan, 1984).

Other patients who consult an analyst might be thought of as individuals suffering from (metaphorical) nightmares, that is, from dreams that are so frightening that they interrupt the psychological work entailed in dreaming both while asleep and in unconscious waking dreaming. (Frost's [1928] phrase "interrupted cry" from his poem, "Acquainted with the night," seems particularly apt in describing a nightmare.[4]) The patient awaking from a nightmare has reached the limits of his capacity for dreaming on his own. He needs the mind of another person – "one acquainted with the night" – to help him dream the yet to be dreamt aspect of his nightmare. (A "yet to be dreamt dream" is a neurotic or other type of non-psychotic phenomenon; an undreamable dream is a psychotic phenomenon or one associated with psychic foreclosure.) The neurotic symptoms manifested by patients with interrupted dreaming represent static stand-ins for the emotional experience that the patient is unable to dream.

The analyst to whom either of these broad categories of people goes for help in dreaming their metaphorical night terrors and nightmares must possess the capacity for reverie, i.e., the capacity to sustain over long periods of time a psychological state of receptivity to the patient's undreamt and interrupted dreams as they are lived out in the transference–countertransference. The analyst's reveries are central to the analytic process in that they constitute a critical avenue through which the analyst participates in dreaming the dreams that the patient is unable to dream on his own.[5]

VI

The patient and analyst engage in an experiment within the terms of the psychoanalytic situation that is designed to generate conditions in which the analysand (with the analyst's participation) may become better able to dream his undreamt and interrupted dreams. The dreams dreamt by the patient and analyst are at the same time their own dreams (and reveries) and those of a third subject who is both and neither patient and analyst.

The experiment that is psychoanalysis is founded upon a paradox. Psychoanalysis is an evolving set of ideas and principles of technique – more a bundle of sticks than a seamless whole – which have been developed over the course of the past century; and yet, at the same time, it is the analyst's responsibility to reinvent psychoanalysis for each patient and continue to reinvent it throughout the course of the analysis. Any mother or father who has had more than one child has learned (with a combination of shock and delight) that each new infant seems to be only a distant relative of his or her older sibling(s). A mother and father must reinvent what it is to be a mother and father with each child and must continue to do so in each phase of the life of the child and the family. Similarly, the analyst must learn anew how to be an analyst with each new patient and in each new session.

While I view psychoanalysis as an experiment, I am not suggesting that patient and analyst are free to do anything they like; rather, they are free to do psychoanalytic work in a way that reflects who they are individually and together *qua analyst and analysand.* That is, they are not inventing a love relationship or a friendship or a religious experience; they are inventing an analytic relationship which has its own psychotherapeutic aims, role definitions, responsibilities, value system, and so on.

Though we cannot predict the nature of the emotional experience that will be generated in the work with a person who consults us, our goal as analysts is very nearly the same with every patient: *the creation of conditions in which the analysand (with the analyst's participation) may become better able to dream his undreamt and interrupted dreams.* While it may seem that the analyst is at first used by the patient to dream the patient's undreamt dreams "by proxy," the analyst's dreams (his reveries in the analytic situation) are from the outset neither solely his own nor those of the patient, but *the dreams of an unconscious third subject who is both and neither patient and analyst* (Ogden, 2003b).

The analytic situation, as I conceive of it, is comprised of three subjects in unconscious conversation with one another: the patient and analyst as separate subjects and the intersubjective "analytic third" (see Ogden 1994a, 1999b for theoretical and clinical discussions of the concept of the analytic third). The unconscious intersubjective "analytic third" is forever in the process of coming into being in the emotional force field generated by the interplay of the unconscious of patient and analyst. The third "subject of analysis" is a subject jointly, but asymmetrically constructed by the analytic pair. When the analytic process is "a going concern" (Winnicott, 1964, p. 27), neither analyst nor analysand may claim to be the sole author of his "own" dreams/reveries.

It is the task of the analyst as separate subject (over time) to become aware of, and to verbally symbolize for himself, his experiences in and of the analytic third. The analyst may eventually speak to the patient *from* that experience *about* his thoughts concerning what is occurring at an unconscious level between himself and the patient. In so doing, the analyst is attempting to engage the patient in a form of conscious thinking that may function in concert with, and may be facilitative of, the patient's unconscious work of dreaming. When, for periods of time, the emotional experience in the intersubjective field is of a subjugating nature, the analytic pair may be unable to think about what is occurring unconsciously between them or to do psychological work with that experience (see Ogden, 1994c, on "the subjugating third").

VII

The psychoanalytic experiment is carried out *within the terms of the psychoanalytic situation*. Central among the terms of the analytic situation is the analyst's conception of analytic methodology, i.e., the analyst's individual conception of analytic theory and principles of technique that he has developed in the course of his experience as an analysand, as a student of psychoanalysis (which is an ongoing aspect of the life of an analyst), and as a practicing analyst. (It is beyond the scope of this chapter to do more than refer to a few of the elements constituting the analyst's methodology.)

Analytic methodology is founded upon the assumption that there is a "differential" (Loewald, 1960, p. 251) between the emotional maturity of the analyst and that of the analysand, i.e., that the analyst has achieved a level of psychological maturity greater than that of the analysand – at least in the areas of experience most troubling to the patient. In addition, it is essential that the analyst be capable of growing emotionally as a consequence of his experience with the patient (in conjunction with his self-analytic work) so that he becomes in the course of the analysis better able to be the analyst that the patient needs him to be (Searles, 1975).

A conception of *how and why* one creates and maintains the features of the "psycho-analytical set-up" (Winnicott, 1954b, p. 278) is critical to one's analytic methodology. The analytic situation usually (but not always) involves the use of the couch, a regular schedule of sessions of a fixed duration, a privileging of emotional expression in the form of words (as opposed to action), and a movement between largely unstructured, freely associative states of mind (on the part of both patient and analyst) and more focused, sequential, secondary process forms of thinking.

A principal subject of the dialogue that takes place in the analytic situation concerns the patient's anxieties and defenses arising in response to the relationship of analyst and analysand at an unconscious level (the transference–countertransference). The transference–countertransference is viewed (in part) from an historical perspective (i.e., from the vantage point of the history of both the life of the patient and the life of the analysis). The analytic situation, though in many ways unstructured, also has a quality of directionality that is derived from the fact that psychoanalysis most fundamentally is a therapeutic enterprise with the goal of enhancing the patient's capacity to be alive to as much as possible of the full spectrum of human experience. Coming to life emotionally is, to my mind, synonymous with becoming increasingly able to dream one's experience, which is to dream oneself into existence.

VIII

In the course of participating in dreaming the patient's undreamt and interrupted dreams, the analyst gets to know the patient in a way and at a depth that may allow him to say something that is true to the conscious and unconscious emotional experience that is occurring in the analytic relationship at that moment. Psychoanalysis centrally involves the analyst's getting to know the patient – a deceptively simple idea – and the patient's coming to feel known by the analyst as well as the patient's feeling that he is getting to know himself and the analyst. In participating in dreaming the patient's undreamt and interrupted dreams, the analyst is not simply coming to understand the patient; he and the patient are together living the previously undreamable or yet-to-be-dreamt emotional experience in the transference–countertransference. In this experience, the patient is in the process of more fully coming into being and the analyst is getting to know the person who the patient is becoming.

Succeeding in getting to know the patient in this way is fraught with difficulty. While the analyst attempts to meet each patient in each new session as if for the first time (Bion, 1978), the analyst's shedding of what he already "knows" requires that he has, in fact, learned from his experience. Only then can he attempt to free himself of what he thought he knew in order to be receptive to all that he does not know (Bion, 1970, 1992; Ogden, 2004a).

The experience of the analyst's getting to know the patient is unique to each analytic encounter, and yet is unavoidably shaped by the particular ways that the analyst has of perceiving and organizing his experience of what is happening, i.e., it is experience viewed through a multifaceted, ever-changing lens informed by one's psychoanalytic ideas and experience. As Wallace Stevens put it, "Things seen are things as seen" (quoted by Vendler, 1997, p. ix).[6] The analyst's experience of getting to know who the patient is becoming is inseparable from the patient's experience of getting to know who the analyst is and is becoming. In my experience, unless the patient feels (with varying degrees of conscious awareness) that he is getting to know his analyst, there is something missing at the core of the analysis: the analytic relationship has become impersonal.

While there is a vast difference between the role of the patient and that of the analyst in the analytic relationship, I do not concur with the idea – often voiced by analysands and defensively fantasized by every analyst at one time or another – that a patient cannot "really" know the analyst because of all that the patient does not know about what is occurring and has occurred in the life of the analyst outside of the analytic situation. What is flawed about this idea, as I see it, is that it does not sufficiently take into account the fact that to the extent that the analyst's life experiences both within and outside of the analytic setting are significant, they genuinely change who the analyst is. That alteration in his being is an unspoken and yet felt presence in the analysis.

To the degree that the analyst is unchanged by a given set of past or current experiences which have occurred within or outside of the analysis, those experiences are either insignificant or the analyst is incapable of being affected by his experience (unable to dream it or learn from it). If the latter is the case, it is doubtful that the analyst is able to engage in genuine analytic work with the patient. Under such circumstances, the patient's statement to the analyst that he cannot "really" get to know the analyst may be the patient's unconscious way of telling the analyst that he (the patient) feels that the analyst is unable to participate either in the process of *getting to know* the patient and himself or of *getting to be known* by the patient. In other words, the patient is feeling that he and the analyst have ceased doing psychoanalysis.

IX

In his effort to *say something to the patient that is true to the conscious and unconscious emotional experience that is occurring in the analytic relationship at a given moment,* the analyst has inevitably, inescapably entered into a struggle with language itself. Awareness of one's feeling states is mediated by words. English professor, Theodore Baird, once asked, "What do you need to fix a motorcycle?" And responded, "You need a language. You need words . . . How do you know it's a motor? . . . Why isn't it a radiator?" (quoted by Varnum, 1996, p. 115). Similarly, one needs language and words to "know" (more accurately, to gain a sense of) what one is feeling (for example, to be able to distinguish among feeling alone, feeling lonely and feeling frightened).

In our effort to use language to convey a sense of what is true to an emotional experience, we find that we cannot say a feeling,[7] but we may be able to say what an emotional experience feels *like*. And for that we need metaphoric language. In the very act of making this transformation from having an emotional experience to saying what it felt like, we are creating not only a new experience, but also a form of self-awareness mediated by verbal symbols (a uniquely human form of consciousness). The enrichment of this form of self-awareness (consciousness) mediated by verbal symbolization is, to my mind, one of the most important aspects of a successful analytic experience.

And yet, while metaphorically putting feelings into words is a necessary component of psychoanalysis, it is not a necessary component of every step or phase of that process. In fact, there are times when the analyst's insistence on using words for communicating experience is antithetical to doing analytic work. Some things unsaid are "far more important than things that are merely said" (Borges, 1970a, p. 211). Borges was referring to his father's unspoken wish that Borges become the writer that Borges' father had aspired to be. In my experience as an analyst and as a supervisor, there are long stretches of time during which the patient's healthy feelings of love for the analyst are a felt presence that is far more important than things "merely said." (This situation is not to be confused with repression, splitting or any other form of avoidance of feeling love.)

X

What the analyst says to the patient regarding what he feels to be true to the emotional situation that is occurring *must be utilizable by the patient for purposes of conscious and unconscious psychological work, i.e., for dreaming his own experience, thereby dreaming himself more fully into existence.* What truth there may be in what the analyst says regarding an emotional experience is of no consequence unless the patient is able to make use of it in doing conscious and unconscious psychological work. For this to occur, the patient must feel known by the analyst in a way that he has never before felt known. The analytic relationship is unique. (The invention of a new form of human relatedness may be Freud's most remarkable contribution to humankind. Being alive in the context of the analytic relationship is different from the experience of being alive in any other form of human relatedness.) Feeling known in the analytic situation is not so much a feeling of being understood as it is a feeling that the analyst knows *who one is.* This is communicated in part through the analyst's speaking to the patient in such a way that what he says and the way he says it could have been spoken by no other analyst to no other patient.

I would hope that if one of my patients were a speck on the wall of my consulting room listening to me work with another patient, the patient-on-the-wall would recognize me as the same person, the same analyst, with whom he is working in analysis, but would find that the way the patient-on-the-couch and I are talking is a way that would not suit the patient-on-the-wall. That way of being together and conversing that is being overheard would feel somehow "off" – perhaps a bit too cerebral or too raw, a bit too serious or too playful, a bit too parental or too spousal. The patient-on-the-wall ideally would not envy the patient-on-the-couch; rather, he would feel that "that is not for me," and of course, he would be right – it is not meant for him.

The interpretations made by an analyst who is wed to a particular "school" of psychoanalysis are frequently addressed to the analyst himself (to his internal and external objects) and not to the patient. When a patient feels that the analyst is speaking in a way that is not meant for him alone, he feels isolated and starved of the opportunity to speak with the analyst about what is true to what is going on in the analysis. I am reminded here of a schizophrenic patient who said to his mother, "You've been just like a mother to me." The analyst who is unable to speak to his patient in a way that has evolved from his experience with *that* patient (and is unique to that patient) is being just like an analyst to the patient.

XI

Now that I have taken apart my initial statement of my conception of psychoanalysis, I will put it together again so that the reader might read it as if for the first time: *A person consults a psychoanalyst because he is in emotional pain, which unbeknownst to him, he is either unable to dream (i.e. unable to do unconscious psychological work) or is so disturbed by what he is dreaming that his dreaming is disrupted. To the extent that he is unable to dream his emotional experience, the individual is unable to change, or to grow, or to become anything other than who he has been. The patient and analyst engage in an experiment within the terms of the psychoanalytic situation that is designed to generate conditions in which the analysand (with the analyst's participation) may become better able to dream his undreamt and interrupted dreams. The dreams dreamt by the patient and analyst are at the same time their own dreams (and reveries) and those of a third subject who is both and neither patient and analyst.*

In the course of participating in dreaming the patient's undreamt and interrupted dreams, the analyst gets to know the patient in a way and at a depth that may allow him to say something to the patient that is true to the conscious and unconscious emotional experience that is occurring in the analytic relationship at a given moment. What the analyst says must be utilizable by the patient for purposes of conscious and unconscious psychological work, i.e. for dreaming his own experience, thereby dreaming himself more fully into existence.

XII Some experiences from the early stages of an analysis

A few days after Mr A and I had set a time to meet for an initial consultation, his secretary called to cancel the meeting for vague reasons having to do with Mr A's business commitments. He called me several weeks later to apologize for the cancellation and to ask to arrange another meeting. In our first session, Mr A, a man in his mid-40s, told me that he had wanted to begin analysis for some time (his wife was currently in analysis), but he had kept putting it off. He quickly added (as if responding to the expectable "therapeutic" question), "I don't know why I was afraid of analysis." He went on, "Although my life looks very good from the outside – I'm successful at my work, I have a very good marriage and three children whom I dearly love – I feel almost all the time that something is terribly wrong." (Mr A's use of the phrases "afraid of analysis," "dearly love," and "terribly wrong" felt to me like anxious unconscious efforts to feign candor while, in fact, telling me almost nothing). I said to Mr A that his having asked his secretary to speak for him made me think that he may feel that his own voice and his own words somehow fail him. Mr A looked at me as if I were crazy and said, "No, my cell phone wasn't working and rather than pay the outrageous amounts that hotels charge for phone calls, I e-mailed my secretary telling her to call you."

During that initial meeting, the patient told me that he suffered from severe insomnia that had begun when he was in college. While trying to fall asleep, he ruminates about all of the things that he has to attend to at work and makes lists in his head of things that need fixing around the house. He added that doctors had prescribed sleeping pills over the years, but "they don't work and I don't want to get hooked on them." (Implicit in his tone was the sentiment: "Doctors do indeed do harm and will get you hooked if you allow them to.")

In the course of the first year-and-a-half of analysis, Mr A told me about his childhood in a rather nostalgic way. He had grown up in a working class suburban neighborhood where he had a group of friends and had done well in school. The patient had put himself through college on scholarships, loans, and long hours of work. He spoke briefly and superficially of his two sisters, one of whom is five years his senior, and the other, two years his junior.

Mr A also talked about his work as director of a non-profit organization that assists illegal immigrants in their dealings with the Immigration and Naturalization Service. He said that when he arrived at work each morning and looked around at the staff and at the clients "camped out" in the lobby, he had to remind himself what he was doing there. (I was not sure what Mr A was doing in my consulting room with me. I was reminded of a story that circulated during my residency: Members of the psychiatric examining board – whatever that was – came to psychiatric clinics posing as patients in order to evaluate the residents and the residency program.)

Mr A very often began his daily sessions by telling me a dream. He said that when he could not remember a dream to tell me, he felt as if he had not done his homework. And yet, when he was able to remember a dream, there was almost always a feeling of letdown on my part as well as his after he told it. It was as if his dreams held no latent content. They were dreams depicting scenes that were almost identical to emotional situations that were regular occurrences in the patient's life. Finding transference (or any other) meanings in the dreams felt like a contrivance in which the patient or I projected "unconscious meaning" into the dream where none existed.

Toward the end of the second year of analysis I became aware of something that may have been going on for some time, but it was only then that it became available to me for conscious psychological work. The rhythm of Mr A's speech was marked by brief, hardly noticeable pauses after almost every sentence, as if preparing himself not to be surprised by me. I said to Mr A that I thought that he was having trouble knowing what to make of me. "It may be that I'm not at all what I seem to be." (My intervention was shaped in part by my observations of the patient's anxious pauses and by my earlier reverie[8] concerning the patient who was not a patient.)

A few weeks after I made this interpretation, it was clear one day when I met Mr A in the waiting room, that he was in great distress. He began by saying that until very recently, he had not really known why he had come to analysis. He had thought it was to please his wife who had been pressuring him to get into analysis. Speaking haltingly, his voice choked with tears, he said, "When I was seven and my younger sister was five, we played doctor. I tried to see into her privates. I wanted to find out what was in there. I used a stick in the way a doctor uses a tongue depressor. I think it happened only two or three times, but I can't be sure. I know it was more than once." At this point Mr A was sobbing and could not speak. After a few minutes, he continued, "I rarely think about it and I've never thought it was a big deal – lots of kids play doctor. I don't know why I only now feel so bad about it. I was up all night last night. I didn't know what I was feeling. I felt sorry for S (he had never used his sister's name before). I don't know if she even remembers it or how it has affected her. I only speak to her on birthdays, Thanksgiving and Christmas." (As Mr A was speaking, I felt moved by the depth of his pain which seemed explosive and utterly unexpected by either of us. It did not seem to me that he was confessing in an effort to elicit forgiveness from me. Rather, it seemed that he was, at least in part, responding to my having interpreted his feeling that he had no idea who I was or what I was up to. He had apparently heard, and been able to make use of the unstated aspect of the interpretation, i.e., that he felt that he had no idea who he was and what he was up to.)

In the months that followed, Mr A began to develop a slight edge of self-awareness that first appeared in the form of a capacity for irony. For example, he opened a session by saying that the high point of his morning had been the warm welcome his auto mechanic had given him when he dropped off his car for the third time in a month for the same problem. He was identifying with me in his use of irony; this had the feel of a boy adopting qualities of his father whom he admires. (Of course, I did not comment on the transference implications of his quip about the mechanic.)

Mr A, as if treading lightly on very dangerous ground, spoke of his life growing up in his childhood family. He was no longer simply a chronicler of romanticized events, but a self-observant person learning from his own verbal renderings of his experience in the very process of his speaking them to me and to himself.

I learned that Mr A's parents owned a shop where they sold and repaired small household appliances – his mother dealt with the customers while his father did the repairs at a workbench at the rear of the store. They were continually on the edge of going out of business. From the time the patient was five, he helped out around the shop and by seven he was doing pick-ups and deliveries. "It wasn't an adventure, it was deadly serious business." Fearful of losing customers, his parents grossly under-charged for their work.

The patient spoke more about his examining his sister's genitals. He said, "She trusted me and went along with me in any game I invented. That's what makes this particularly ugly, the way I took advantage of her trust. I have no excuses that are worth anything to me." I said to Mr A, "It seems to me that you're trying to face the music." (Only after having used the phrase "face the music," did I hear its double meaning: In facing the music, one dares to take on the reality of what is [as a fearful actor must do in facing the audience across the orchestra pit]; and at the same time, there is a beauty [music] to the experience of being honest with oneself, even though one is powerless to undo what one has done.)

In the session that followed, Mr A told me that the previous night he had had a dream that was a sort of dream he had dreamt many times before (he had never told me about these dreams). "It takes place in the lobby of a movie theater with big posters in glass cases. There is a popcorn and candy stand with lots of customers standing in line. But then I realize with horror that the theater is completely deserted and has been shut down for years. This time – and it's happened a couple of times before – I refuse to believe that what I had seen wasn't real. I woke up from the dream with my heart racing, not with fear, but with anger." I said to Mr A, "In your dream, you hold on to your own perceptions, not to prove you're right, but to prove you are who you are." (My interpretation felt hackneyed and dangerously close to something one might read in a self-help book. Fortunately, Mr A was able to do his own psychological work here in spite of me.) The patient responded in a loud, angry voice that I had not previously heard, "The movie theater *worked* as a movie theater – that's not asking too much is it?" (I felt that some of Mr A's outrage was directed at me for my impersonal intervention.) And then, more softly, he added, "I was ashamed of my parents and of myself. I wished – and still do wish – that they had been like my friends' parents who, even though they didn't have any more money than my parents, didn't behave like animals who had all the life beaten out of them. I feel bad talking about my parents this way." I said, "It's a complicated thing: even at the beginning of the dream, when you thought everything worked as it should, it was at the cost of being alone with it." (I thought but did not say that he was furious at his parents, not only for their being what he felt to be shameful failures, but also for their inability, even for a moment, to dream with him something exciting, however improbable it might be.)

Mr A and I were silent for several minutes during which a subtle shift occurred that I recognized only in retrospect. During that silence my thoughts wandered to a film that I had seen in which an actress whom I like very much is the main character. In that film I found her particularly charming and sexy. It

14

was not the character she played to whom I felt drawn, it was to her, the actress, the woman I imagined her to be. In the film she sang two songs and I was amazed not only by the beauty of the sound of her voice, but also by the enormous range of her talent.

The patient told me later in the session that from the time his daughter was a baby, it had been impossible for him to hold her in his arms in a way that felt natural, much less change her diaper without feeling that he was "being a voyeur and a pervert." As Mr A was speaking, my mind turned from the images and feelings associated with the patient's having played doctor with his sister to an event from my own experience of becoming a doctor. In the early weeks of medical school – I was twenty-one at the time, I defensively noted to myself – my group of four medical students was working on the dissection of "our" cadaver. I remembered having lived with a great deal of fear during that period of my life.

The four of us were all business in the dissection, each alone with his terrors. There was a moment when feelings seemed to break through the guise of the ardent, confident students of medicine: We began talking to the cadaver addressing him by an invented first name as if he were alive but too shy to talk. I remembered having felt at the time that this joke was a dangerous one, as if we were violating a sacred law. At the same time, the joke, which was full of anger and fear, was a welcome release.

As I was recalling these feelings and events, I felt a deep sense of having betrayed a trust. The cadaver had been a middle-aged man, probably about my current age when he died, a man who had been generous in donating his body for medical education and research. He did not deserve to be treated like a dummy in a vaudeville act. I felt a combination of guilt in connection with what I had done and compassion for myself as a young man who was doing the best he could in the face of emotional events too disturbing to be borne alone and too shameful to be admitted to anyone else. I could still smell the thick odor of formaldehyde that had filled the room in which the twenty-three cadavers had been laid out on their stainless steel tables. It was an odor that was always with me because it had soaked into my clothes and into my skin. As a medical student, unable to dream this experience, I had developed a mild psychosomatic disorder. It was an undreamable emotional experience that required considerable analytic work on my part in order for me to begin to be able to dream the foreclosed thoughts and feelings.

As my attention shifted from this reverie back to Mr A, a particular aspect of what Mr A had said recently about his childhood took on enhanced meaning for me. His mother's only friends had been her two sisters and she had made no effort to hide the fact that they were far more important to her than was the patient's father. Neither did she disguise the fact that it was the patient's older sister who captivated her in a way that the patient and his younger sister did not. Although Mr A did not say so explicitly, it seemed to me at this point that his mother had used the patient's older sister as a vehicle through whom to live the life of a girl, and then of a young woman, who she wished she had been. (I began to recognize that earlier in the analysis, I had too readily adopted as my own the patient's view of his parents as defeated people utterly lacking in dreams. It now seemed that it was Mr A's father who had been the defeated one and that the patient's depiction of his mother as a person without dreams had served to protect him from the even more disturbing feeling that his [external and internal object] mother had been alive – albeit primarily narcissistically – to his older sister, but not to him.)

Later in the session, Mr A spoke about his inadequacies as a husband including his feeling that he is "lousy at sex": "It's like dancing. I have no sense of rhythm and I try to move my body in the way other people do, but it's not dancing. I don't feel the music." I said to the patient, "I think you felt that you'd never be able to dance with your mother in the way your older sister did. It was only something girls and women knew about." (In retrospect, I believe that this interpretation was derived in part from my reverie concerning the actress who could do everything, including sing beautifully. Although I had not been aware of it at the time that the reverie occurred, I realized at this point in the session that I had not only been admiring of the actress, I had been envious of her for being a woman. Both the patient and I were unconsciously giving metaphoric shape to our experience of being inadequate because we would never be a girl or a woman who could captivate his mother. Both my reverie concerning the music of the actress's singing and my use of the phrase "face the music" were parts of the unconscious context for the patient's use of music as a metaphor for his own feelings of inadequacy for not having been born a girl and for lacking whatever else it would have taken to have won his mother's love.)

In response to my comment about his feeling invisible to his mother, the patient said, "In a way even now I feel that there's something impenetrable about women and their ties to one another. They live in a whole other reality unknowable by a man. I don't have words for it – they live inside their bodies, not on the surface of their bodies the way men do. Their pocket books are like pouches in which they carry around their secrets. I don't really believe that men, with their simple-minded uncomplicated penises, have anything to do with the mystery of making a baby. A woman's body is strange, in a way grotesque, with amazing powers."

Mr A's comments led me to think further about parts of my reverie experience. I began to be aware of a facet of meaning of the medical school reverie that I had not previously recognized. I had been feeling the unbridgeable void between me and the person on the anatomy table. He was human; I could see and touch his face and hands. He had small, delicate hands. And yet, it, the cadaver, was a thing. I had felt deeply disturbed by my inability to reconcile the two: he was there in all his humanness, his generosity, and at the same time, there was no one there, he was absolutely, irretrievably dead, merely a thing with whom no human connection could be made. Perhaps "the joke," for me, had been a futile effort to mitigate the absolute quality of that divide.

My experience of dissecting the cadaver as it was taking place had held a great many powerful meanings for me, including frighteningly immediate confrontations with my own mortality, terrors associated with bodily mutilation, and feelings of loss of my capacities to feel (to remain emotionally alive) in the face of an experience that shook me to the core. However, in the analytic session with Mr A that I am discussing, specific aspects of that set of experiences took on particular importance as dreamt, incompletely dreamt and undreamt aspects of my own psychological pain. In order to do analytic work with Mr A, it was necessary for me to make use of the unconscious experience with him as an opportunity to dream (in the form of reverie experience) some of my own "night terrors" and "nightmares" that overlapped with his. It is impossible to say whether the disturbing gap between me and the cadaver was part of the original medical school experience or was an emotional experience generated for the first time in the context of my work with Mr A.

A month or so after the session I have just described, Mr A and his family took a three-week vacation trip to Asia. On his return, Mr A told me that something very important had occurred during the time that he was away. He said that he had taken some instruction in Buddhist thought and meditation and had "experienced a connection with something greater than myself in a way I have never felt before." Mr A went on to speak at some length about the transformation that he had undergone. He no longer seemed to be speaking in a way that was specific to me (as he had in the sessions prior to the vacation break). I was not at all surprised when he eventually told me that he had decided to pursue Buddhist meditation and so this would be our last session. The rhythm of the movement of the analysis at this point had the feel of a disruption of dreaming.

I was aware practically from the start of Mr A's telling me about his response to Buddhism that I was being cast in the role of the outsider who did not have the slightest chance of competing with the enormous emotional power of Mr A's new (narcissistic object) love. An unbridgeable divide between the two of us had been created. I said to the patient, "I won't try to talk you out of what you have in mind to do [i.e., I would not act out with him the humiliation of begging for his mother's love in the face of the impenetrable narcissistic self-involvement that he had encountered in her]. What I will do is what you and I always do and that is to put into words what's going on" (i.e., I would remain myself, his analyst, even in the face of his threatening to isolate himself from me in narcissism while projecting into me the loneliness and impotence that he could not bear to experience on his own).

I continued, "It seems to me that I have a responsibility both to you, the person with whom I am talking, and to you, the person who originally came to see me, the person who, without knowing it, was asking me for my help in facing the music. I am responsible to both aspects of you despite the fact that, for the moment, one of them is mute and I must do the talking for that aspect of you" (i.e., I would not repeat with him the childhood scene of his mother's embracing one of her children and discarding the others).

In the session that followed, Mr A and I spoke about the fear he had felt of losing himself and me during the vacation break. He said that, despite the fact that in the past he had asked me to fill his sessions when he is away, he had hoped that I would know that this time I should keep them for him. "They're my times and it wouldn't feel right to have someone else here."

A bit later in that session, Mr A told me, "When I left here yesterday, it felt like a weight had been lifted . . . no that's not it . . . I felt that I'd come back to myself and coming back to myself isn't entirely a good thing, as you know. It's been a place that's been unbearable to be. It was good to hear your voice while you were speaking yesterday – I listened more to the sound of your voice than to what you were saying. It wasn't just the sound of your voice, it was the sound of you thinking. When I could hear that your voice hadn't changed, I knew that you hadn't given my place away. It doesn't matter whether you really have or haven't filled the times – I know you know that." (There was a feeling of profound affection and gratitude in Mr A's voice as he spoke that I had not heard before – and I have no doubt that he knew I knew that too.)

It seemed to me at this juncture in the analysis that Mr A's molestation of his sister represented an acting out of intense sets of feelings that he had experienced as a child and were currently being experienced in the transference–countertransference. His repeatedly looking into his sister's genitals seemed to me to represent an attempt to find out what was "in there" (inside his mother's body and mind), which was at once "grotesque" and "with amazing powers." The patient may have imagined that what he found "in there" would hold the key to the mysterious emotional bond that tied his mother so strongly to her sisters and to his older sister. The molestations may also have represented angry attacks on, and forced entries into, his mother's genitals and insides in retaliation for what he felt to be her almost complete emotional exclusion of him. And finally – and perhaps most important – the patient may have been attempting to find his place "in there," a place that was meant only for him, a place that could never be taken away from him and given to someone else.

In the weeks and months that followed, as different facets of this constellation of internal object relationships came to life in the transference–countertransference, Mr A and I thought and spoke and dreamt these emotional experiences.

2

What I would not part with

I could give all to Time except – except
What I myself have held. But why declare
The things forbidden that while the Customs slept
I have crossed to Safety with? For I am There,
And what I would not part with I have kept.

(Frost, 1942b, pp. 304–305)

Paradoxically, in the analytic setting, the analyst attempts not to be judgmental; and yet, he must bring to the situation values that provide the underpinning of analytic work, values that he "would not part with." When I speak of analytic values, what I have in mind is not a psychoanalytic morality nor a code of ethical conduct; neither am I referring to a set of concepts that I believe to be essential to psychoanalysis (for example, the notion of the dynamic unconscious, transference and defense). Rather, in speaking of psychoanalytic values, I am referring to those ways of being and ways of seeing that characterize the distinctive manner in which each of us practices psychoanalysis. In this chapter I will attempt to convey to the reader the values that lie at the core of the way I practice psychoanalysis, and of who I am as a psychoanalyst.

I Being humane

Each element of an analytic value system is inseparable from all of the others, and yet, to my mind, there is a hierarchy of importance among the elements of that system. For me, what is most fundamental to psychoanalysis is the principle that an analyst treats his patient – and all those his patient's life impinges upon – in a humane way, in a way that at all times honors human dignity. This principle is the North Star of psychoanalysis; it is a point of reference in terms of which all else is located. When an analyst is not being humane, what he is doing with the patient is not recognizable to me as psychoanalysis.

19

Being humane in the psychoanalytic setting is more easily illustrated in its breach than in its fulfillment. For example, I believe that it is inhumane for an analyst to abruptly discontinue the analysis of a patient by explaining to the patient that the patient's having developed a serious physical illness has made his problems "real" and therefore not amenable to psychoanalytic work. Another form of inhumane behavior on the part of the analyst involves his treating the patient's psychological illness as a moral failing that warrants the analyst's scorn (as expressed, for instance, by loudly opening and reading his mail as the patient is speaking).

The analyst recognizes that a patient's inhumane behavior (often directed against himself) is usually a reflection of the psychological illness for which he came to the analyst for help. The analyst neither condones the patient's inhumane behavior (for example, the patient's relentless self-debasing thoughts and actions or his burning himself with cigarettes), nor does he respond to the patient with an expression of revulsion. Rather, he treats the behavior as an urgent plea for the analyst's aid. Up to a point the analyst responds by engaging in conscious and unconscious psychological work in which the patient's inhumane behavior is treated as an unconscious communication. There reaches a point, however, when the way in which the patient is communicating his pain is so cruel (to himself, to the analyst or to others) that it would be unconscionable for the analyst to proceed with "analysis as usual."

I believe that there is no such entity as psychoanalysis under conditions in which the analyst allows extreme inhumanity on the part of the patient to take place, such as leaving very young children unattended for long periods of time or torturing animals to death. Under such circumstances, it is incumbent upon the analyst not to cease being a psychoanalyst, but to become a psychoanalyst doing something else (Winnicott, 1962). When a patient's inhumane behavior reaches an unacceptable level, the analyst must treat the situation as an emergency requiring decisive action. By behaving in this way, the analyst shows the patient, in an unselfrighteous way, who the analyst is, what matters most to him (and, by implication what is important to the values inherent in psychoanalysis).

Being humane in the analytic setting is not synonymous with diminishing the patient's psychological pain (unless the pain reaches unbearable proportions or duration); psychological pain is necessary to the analytic process. Pain marks the path and determines the sequence of the psychological work that needs to be done. The patient's effort to make psychological change is inherently frightening and painful, for it means giving up ways of protecting himself that in infancy and childhood had felt to be critical to his effort to maintain his sanity (and hence, his very survival). Those ways of being that the patient had felt, and continues unconsciously to feel, necessary for his sanity/survival are also what severely limits the ways in which he is able to live his life. Often the patient unconsciously, ambivalently consults the analyst for help with this dilemma – the incompatibility of safety and generativity.

As I view it, an analyst continues to be an analyst when engaged in forms of relatedness to the patient that are not viewed as "standard psychoanalysis," e.g., visiting a seriously ill patient in the hospital or attending a memorial service for the patient's wife. (I have had occasion to experience the former analytic event.) Such interventions, when preceded by thoughtful consideration and (when possible) discussion with the patient have been – in my experience as an analysand, an analyst and a supervisor – some of the most important events in an analysis. These interventions are not of analytic value simply because they are humane; they are of analytic value because they are both humane and facilitative of significant conscious and unconscious psychological work.

II Facing the music

Among the ways of being that I value in the analytic setting, perhaps second in importance only to the analyst's being humane, is the effort on the part of the analyst and the patient to face the truth, to be honest with themselves in the face of disturbing emotional experience. Doing so is one of the most difficult of human tasks. This striving to face the truth lies at the heart of the analytic process and gives it direction. In the absence of the effort on the part of patient and analyst to "face the music," what occurs in the analysis has a shallow, desultory, as-if quality to it.

I view psychoanalysis as most fundamentally an effort by patient and analyst to put into words what is true to the patient's emotional experience. This articulation holds such great importance because the very act of thinking and giving "shape" to what is true to the patient's emotional experience alters that truth. This perspective underlies my conception of the therapeutic action of interpretation: in interpreting, the analyst verbally symbolizes what he intuits to be true to the patient's unconscious experience and, in so doing, alters what is true and contributes to the creation of a potentially new experience with which the analytic pair may do psychological work.

Patient and analyst are not in search of truth for its own sake; they are principally interested in what is true to what is happening in the transference–countertransference. The analytic pair is doing so for the purpose of creating a containing human context in which the patient may be able to live with his past and present emotional experience (as opposed to evacuating it or deadening himself to it).

In helping the patient to face the truth of his emotional experience, the analyst is respectful of the ways the patient (beginning in his infancy) has found to protect his sanity. The rhythm and pace of the patient's efforts to face the truth of his emotional experience is set by the patient. A large part of the analyst's role involves holding the tension between the patient's need for safety and his need for truth.

III Being accountable

The analyst holds himself responsible for his own behavior and holds the patient responsible for his (the patient's). Accountability does not end at the edge of one's conscious control over oneself. That is, the analyst holds himself responsible for behaving seductively or jealously or competitively or arrogantly with the patient regardless of whether he is conscious of doing so at the time or had it in his power to refrain from doing so. Similarly, the patient is held responsible, for example, for his being verbally abusive to his wife whether or not his behavior is within his conscious control at the moment he is doing it. Moreover, we ask of ourselves (and of the patient) that over time there be an increase in the degree of control exercised over such behavior and an increase in the degree of conscious awareness of the previously unconscious context for the behavior.

The analyst's responsibility is not to "psychoanalysis," but to the welfare of the patient. The patient has come to him – though often unaware of it – not "to be analyzed," but for help in doing the psychological work that he needs to do in order to live his life differently. Living differently may mean living in a way that is less tormented, or less lonely, or less empty, or less devoid of a sense of self, or less destructive, or less selfish. The analyst's aim is not to carry out the dictates of a set of analytic rules (often codified by the analytic school to which he "belongs"), but to attend analytically to the patient's human dilemma.

The analyst not only lives and works within the terms of the analytic situation, he also lives and works in the context of the social/political situation of his time. (David Rosenfeld's [2004] analytic work during and following the "disappearances" under the military dictatorships in Argentina and the Pinochet regime in Chile bears witness to the weight borne by the analyst in recognizing and being alive to both the patient's individual psychological state and the external social context.) The analyst is responsible not only for remaining receptive and responsive to the truth of what is occurring in the consulting room, but also to what is true to what is happening in the outside world. The analyst does not necessarily directly address the current social/political realities of the time, and certainly does not attempt to convince, debate or proselytize; but there is an "ethical instinct, [a sense of] when [one] must do good" (Borges, 1975, p. 412) that he embodies in the analysis. What Robert Pinsky (1988) writes concerning the responsibilities of the poet holds important bearing on the forms of responsibility carried by the psychoanalyst. The poet, for Pinsky,

> needs not so much an audience, as to feel a need to answer, a promise to respond. The promise may be a contradiction, it may be unwanted, it may go unheeded . . . but it is owed, and the sense that it is owed is a basic requirement for the poet's good feeling about the art. The need to answer, as firm as a borrowed object or a cash debt is the ground where the centaur [the imagination] walks.
>
> (p. 85)

While the analyst ordinarily does not make his social/political views known to the patient, his "promise [to himself] to respond," his "ethical instinct" is a felt presence in the analysis as the patient wrestles with his own complex set of kept and unkept promises to himself concerning his efforts to face and respond (in both thought and action) to what it is true to his internal and external worlds.

IV Dreaming oneself into being

The patient's psychological growth, as I view it, involves the expansion of his capacity to experience the full range of his emotional experience, his "joys and griefs, and . . . shipwreck too" (Goethe, 1808, p. 46). Randall Jarrell (1955) describes this span of feeling in Frost's poetry:

> To have the distance from the most awful and most nearly unbearable parts
> of the poems, to the most tender, subtle and loving parts, a distance so great;
> to have this whole range of being treated with so much humor and sadness
> and composure, with such plain truth; to see that a man can still include,
> connect, and make humanly understandable or humanly ununderstandable
> so *much* – this is one of the freshest and oldest of joys.
>
> (p. 62)

A psychoanalyst must be able to recognize with sadness and compassion that among the worst and most crippling of human losses is the loss of the capacity to be alive to one's experience – in which case one has lost a part of one's humanness. The awful reality (which is never entirely a psychic reality) that lies at the source of such a catastrophe may involve the patient's having been deprived in infancy and childhood of the opportunity to receive and give love. For others, it may have its source in experiences of unimaginable, unspeakable pain such as that experienced in concentration camps or in the death of one's child – pain so terrible that it is beyond the capacity of a human being to both take it in and remain fully emotionally alive.

Being alive to one's experience is, as I conceive of it, synonymous with being able to dream one's lived emotional experience. I am using the term *dreaming* here in a way that is informed by Bion's (1962a) work. To the extent that one is capable of dreaming one's experience, one is able to generate an emotional response to it, learn from it, and be changed by it.

As discussed in the previous chapter, I believe that central to psychoanalysis is the analyst's participation in dreaming the patient's "undreamt" and "inter-rupted" dreams. Interrupted dreams (metaphorical nightmares) are emotional experiences with which the patient is able to do genuine unconscious psycho-logical work. However, the patient's dreaming (his unconscious psychological work) is disrupted at a point where the capacity for dreaming is overwhelmed

23

by the disturbing nature of what is being dreamt. At that point the patient "wakes up," i.e., ceases to be able to continue doing unconscious psychological work. We observe this phenomenon in a child's sudden play disruption that occurs when the content of the play becomes so distressing that it overwhelms the capacity for playing (the child sweeps off the table all of the figures with which he had been engrossed).

In contrast to interrupted dreams, undreamt dreams are emotional experiences with which the patient is unable to do any unconscious psychological work. Undreamable experience is held in psychologically split-off states such as pockets of autism or psychosis, psychosomatic disorders and severe perversions. Undreamt dreams are comparable to night terrors in that the latter are not genuine dreams (they occur in non-REM sleep) and achieve no psychological work; the "dreamer" does not awaken from them and in a sense only awakens if he is eventually able to dream the formerly undreamable emotional experience. Undreamt dreams remain amorphous, ominous, unimaginable threats to one's sanity and one's very being. (Winnicott [1967] described this sense of foreboding as a "fear of breakdown.")

To dream one's experience is to make it one's own in the process of dreaming, thinking and feeling it. The continuity of one's being – the background "hum" of being alive – is the continuous "sound" of one's dreaming oneself into being. Psychoanalysis, from this vantage point, is a form of psychological relatedness in which the analyst participates in the patient's dreaming his previously undreamt and interrupted dreams. The goal of psychoanalysis is not simply the dreaming of the patient's undreamt and interrupted dreams in the analytic setting. The analyst's participating in dreaming the patient's previously undreamable experience is a means to an end: the patient's development of his capacity to dream his experience on his own. The end of an analytic experience is measured not so much by the degree of resolution of intrapsychic conflict as it is by the degree to which the patient has become able to dream his experience on his own.

V Thinking out loud

Critical to a successful analytic experience is the development of the use of language that is adequate to the task of communicating to oneself and to others something of what one is feeling and thinking. There is no ideal form for the analytic dialogue. Quite the contrary, the way analyst and analysand speak to one another is something that they must invent for themselves. When analysis is a "going concern" (Winnicott, 1964, p. 27), their invention is unique.

When analyst and analysand are able to think and speak for themselves, they do not use "borrowed language," e.g., jargon, cliché and technical terms. Their language tends to be alive, their metaphors freshly minted and unassuming.

Their use of language serves to communicate, not obfuscate; to generate understandings, not confusion; to say what is true to one's emotional experience, not to pervert the truth.

The analyst, when talking to a patient in his own voice, does not sound "like an analyst"; his voice is that of an ordinary person speaking to another ordinary person in a way that is personal to the other person and to the history of their relationship. A quality that often characterizes this kind of analytic dialogue is the feeling that the analyst and analysand are each finding out what · he thinks in the very act of speaking. I find that I rarely know how I am going · to end a sentence or what the next sentence will be when I begin talking to a · patient.

While psychoanalysis depends heavily on the use of language, talking and self-reflective thinking are not enough to sustain a generative analytic experience. What the patient and analyst think and say must be tied directly or indirectly to the patient's emotional growth, growth that is reflected in action, i.e., to actual changes in the way the patient lives his life, in the way he conducts himself in the world. Otherwise, thinking and talking – however insightful they may be – are mere mental gymnastics; the patient and analyst are involved in a simulation of psychoanalysis.

VI Not knowing

Psychoanalysis – significantly shaped by Bion over the past quarter century – has come to place great value on the analyst's and the analysand's capacity not to know. In this state of mind, one is capable of marveling at the mystery, the utter unpredictability, and the power of the unconscious which can be felt, but never known. The unconscious is an immanence, not an oracle.

When an analyst is incapable of sustaining a state of "not knowing," the past eclipses the present, and the present is projected into the future. An analyst unable to tolerate not knowing may "know" even before the analysand arrives for his Monday session that the patient – as he has so often in the past – has felt lonely and intensely jealous of the analyst's (imagined) wife. What's more, the patient once again will feel that the analyst cruelly flaunts the patient's exclusion from his family by having his consulting room in his home. The patient may in fact have felt all of this, but in order for that set of feelings to be talked about in a way that is personal to the patient, the patient's experience must be sensed by the analyst and spoken about as if for the first time. For the event is in fact occurring for the first time in the context of the unique present moment of the analysis.

The analyst must be able *not to know* himself too well. For example, the analyst's eight-year-old son may have been in a bicycle accident the previous day in which the boy had broken his arm. The analyst's awareness of the fact that he is still strongly reacting to the event is only a starting point since the meanings of the event are many and are still in the process of being generated. Only by not knowing the meaning of his thoughts and feelings about his child's accident will the analyst be able to discern the way in which his experience of that event is different with each patient and that his thoughts and feelings regarding his child are generated freshly with each patient and shaped by what is happening in each session. For example, with one patient the analyst's reveries may center on a conversation with the orthopedist in which the analyst felt ashamed of his wish to be treated as a medical colleague by the doctor; with another patient, the analyst's reveries may take the form of fears about the possibility that his son's fracture will result in permanent limitation of arm movement; and with still another patient, the analyst may feel a mixture of sadness and admiration as he remembers the courage that his son had shown in telling the doctor (in a very sweet way) about how he had gone about deciding to go home and not to go to his friend's house after the accident, even though the friend's house was much closer by.

Each of these various reveries unconsciously makes use of the analyst's emotional experience with his son in a way that is a product of what is happening at an unconscious level (at a given moment) between himself and a particular patient. The experience of the accident and its sequelae are no longer the sole possession of the analyst. They have become an experience of "the analytic third" (Ogden, 1994a, 1997b), a subject co-created by patient and analyst whose thoughts and feelings are experienced by the analyst in a form of waking dreaming (i.e., his reveries).

Not knowing is a precondition for being able to imagine. The imaginative capacity in the analytic setting is nothing less than sacred. Imagination holds open multiple possibilities experimenting with them all in the form of thinking, playing, dreaming and in every other sort of creative activity. Imagination stands in contrast to fantasy which has a fixed form that is repeated again and again and goes nowhere (for example, as seen in sexual impotence derived from fantasies that sex is lethal to oneself or one's sexual partner). To imagine is not to figure out a solution to an emotional problem; it is to change the very terms of the dilemma. For instance, a patient may feel that he must choose between maintaining his own sanity and being loved by his mother. To alter the terms of this human dilemma may take the form of recognizing that love that requires giving up one's mind is a form of love that is impersonal in that it obliterates who one is.

The analytic values that I have discussed together comprise for me a bedrock, "what I would not part with" in practicing psychoanalysis. The reader will have his own analytic values derived from his experience. For me, these values are "the very ground where the [psychoanalytic] centaur walks" (Pinsky, 1988, p. 85), the living soul of psychoanalysis.

3

A new reading of the origins of object relations theory

Some writers write what they think; others think what they write. The latter seem to do their thinking in the very act of writing, as if thoughts arise from the conjunction of pen and paper, the work unfolding by surprise as it goes. Freud in many of his most important books and articles, including "Mourning and melancholia" (1917b), was a writer of this latter sort. In these writings, Freud made no attempt to cover his tracks, for example, his false starts, his uncertainties, his reversals of thinking (often done mid-sentence), his shelving of compelling ideas for the time being because they seemed to him too speculative or lacking adequate clinical foundation.

The legacy that Freud left was not simply a set of ideas, but as important, and inseparable from those ideas, a new way of thinking about human experience that gave rise to nothing less than a new form of human subjectivity. Each of his psychoanalytic writings, from this point of view, is simultaneously an explication of a set of concepts and a demonstration of a newly created way of thinking about and experiencing ourselves.

I have chosen to look closely at Freud's "Mourning and melancholia" for two reasons. First, I consider this paper to be one of Freud's most important contributions in that it develops for the first time, in a systematic way, a line of thought which later would be termed "object relations theory"[1] (Fairbairn, 1952). This line of thought has played a major role in shaping psychoanalysis from 1917 onward. Second, I have found that attending closely to Freud's writing *as writing* in "Mourning and melancholia" provides an extraordinary opportunity not only to listen to Freud think, but also, through the writing, to enter into that thinking process with him. In this way, the reader may learn a good deal about what is distinctive to the new form of thinking (and its attendant subjectivity) that Freud was in the process of creating in this article.[2]

Freud wrote "Mourning and melancholia" in less than three months in early 1915 during a period that was for him filled with great intellectual and emotional upheaval. Europe was in the throes of World War I. Despite his protestations, two of Freud's sons volunteered for military service and fought at the front lines. Freud was at the same time in the grips of intense intellectual foment. In the years 1914 and 1915, Freud wrote a series of 12 essays which represented his first major revision of psychoanalytic theory since the publication of *The Interpretation of Dreams* (1900). Freud's intent was to publish these papers as a book to be titled *Preliminaries to a Metapsychology*. He hoped that this collection would "provide a stable theoretical foundation for psycho-analysis" (Freud, quoted by Strachey, 1957, p. 105).

In the summer of 1915, Freud wrote to Ferenczi, "The twelve articles are, as it were, ready" (Gay, 1988, p. 367). As the phrase "as it were" suggests, Freud had misgivings about what he had written. Only five of the essays – all of which are ground-breaking papers – were ever published: "Instincts and their vicis-situdes," "Repression," and "The unconscious" were published as journal articles in 1915. "A metapsychological supplement to the theory of dreams" and "Mourning and melancholia," although completed in 1915, were not published until 1917. Freud destroyed the other seven articles which papers he told Ferenczi "deserved suppression and silence" (Gay, 1988, p. 373). None of these articles was shown to even his innermost circle of friends. Freud's reasons for "silencing" these essays remain a mystery in the history of psychoanalysis.

In the discussion that follows, I take up five portions of the text of "Mourning and melancholia," each of which contains a pivotal contribution to the analytic understanding of the unconscious work of mourning and of melancholia; at the same time, I look at the way Freud made use of this seemingly focal exploration of these two psychological states as a vehicle for introducing – as much implicitly as explicitly – the foundations of his theory of unconscious internal object relations.[3]

I

Freud's unique voice resounds in the opening sentence of "Mourning and melancholia":

> Dreams having served us as the prototype in normal life of narcissistic mental disorders, we will now try to throw some light on the nature of melancholia by comparing it with the normal affect of mourning.
>
> (1917b, p. 243)

The voice we hear in Freud's writing is remarkably constant through the twenty-three volumes of the *Standard Edition*. It is a voice with which no other psychoanalyst has written because no other analyst has had the right to do so. The voice Freud creates is that of the founding father of a new discipline.[4] Already in this opening sentence, something quite remarkable can be heard which we regularly take for granted in reading Freud: in the course of the twenty years preceding the writing of this sentence, Freud had not only created a revolutionary conceptual system, he had altered language itself. It is for me astounding to observe that virtually every word in the opening sentence has acquired in Freud's hands, new meanings and a new set of relationships, not only to practically every other word in the sentence, but also to innumerable words in language as a whole. For example, the word "dreams" that begins the sentence is a word that conveys rich layers of meaning and mystery that did not exist prior to the publication of *The Interpretation of Dreams* (1900). Concentrated in this word newly created by Freud are allusions to (1) a conception of a repressed unconscious inner world that powerfully, but obliquely exerts force on conscious experience, and vice versa; (2) a view that sexual desire is present from birth onward and is rooted in bodily instincts which manifest themselves in universal unconscious incestuous wishes, parricidal fantasies and fears of retaliation in the form of genital mutilation; (3) a recognition of the role of dreaming as an essential conversation between unconscious and preconscious aspects of ourselves; and (4) a radical reconceptualization of human symbology – at once universal and exquisitely idiosyncratic to the life history of each individual. Of course, this list is only a sampling of the meanings that the word "dream" – newly made by Freud – invokes.

Similarly, the words "normal life," "mental disorders," and "narcissistic" speak to one another and to the word "dream" in ways that simply could not have occurred twenty years earlier. The second half of the sentence suggests that two other words denoting aspects of human experience will be made anew in this paper: "mourning" and "melancholia."[5]

The logic of the central argument of "Mourning and melancholia" begins to unfold as Freud compares the psychological features of mourning to those of melancholia: both are responses to loss and involve "grave departures from the normal attitude to life" (p. 243).[6] In melancholia, one finds

> a profoundly painful dejection, cessation of interest in the outside world, loss of the capacity to love, inhibition of all activity, and a lowering of the self-regarding feelings to a degree that finds utterance in self-reproaches and self-revilings, and culminates in a delusional expectation of punishment.
>
> (Freud, 1917b, p. 244)

Freud points out that the same traits characterize mourning – with one exception: "the disturbance of self-regard." Only in retrospect will the reader realize that the full weight of the thesis that Freud develops in this paper rests on this simple observation made almost in passing: "The disturbance of self-regard is absent in mourning; but otherwise the features are the same" (p. 244). As in every good detective novel, all clues necessary for solving the crime are laid out in plain view practically from the outset.

With the background of the discussion of the similarities and differences – there is only one symptomatic difference – between mourning and melancholia, the paper seems abruptly to plunge into the exploration of the unconscious. In melancholia, the patient and the analyst may not even know what the patient has lost – a remarkable idea from the point of view of common sense in 1915. Even when the melancholic is aware that he has suffered the loss of a person, "he knows *whom* he has lost but not *what* he has lost in him" (p. 245). There is ambiguity in Freud's language here: is the melancholic unaware of the sort of importance the tie to the object held for him: "*what* [the melancholic] has lost in [losing] him." Or is the melancholic unaware of what he has lost *in himself* as a consequence of losing the object? The ambiguity – whether or not Freud intended it – subtly introduces the important notion of the simultaneity and interdependence of two unconscious aspects of object loss in melancholia. One involves the nature of the melancholic's tie to the object and the other involves an alteration of the self in response to the loss of the object.

> This [lack of awareness on the part of the melancholic of what he has lost] would suggest that melancholia is in some way related to an object-loss which is withdrawn from consciousness, in contradistinction to mourning, in which there is nothing about the loss that is unconscious.
>
> (p. 245)

In his effort to understand the nature of the unconscious object-loss in melancholia, Freud returns to the sole observable symptomatic difference between mourning and melancholia: the melancholic's diminished self-esteem.

> In mourning it is the world which has become poor and empty; in melan-cholia it is the ego itself. The patient represents his ego to us as worthless, incapable of any achievement and morally despicable; he reproaches himself, vilifies himself and expects to be cast out and punished. He abases him-self before everyone and commiserates with his own relatives for being connected with anyone so unworthy. He is not of the opinion that a change has taken place in him, but extends his self-criticism back over the past; he declares that he was never any better.
>
> (p. 246)

More in his use of language than in explicit theoretical statements, Freud's model of the mind is being re-worked here. There is a steady flow of subject–object, I–me pairings in this passage: the patient as subject reproaches, abases, vilifies himself as object (and extends the reproaches backward and forward in time). What is being suggested – and only suggested – is that these subject–object pairings extend beyond consciousness into the timeless unconscious and constitute what is going on unconsciously in melancholia that is not occurring in mourning. The unconscious is in this sense a metaphorical place in which the "I–me" pairings are unconscious psychological contents that actively engage in a continuous timeless attack of the subject (I) upon the object (me) which depletes the ego (a concept in transition here) to the point that it becomes "poor and empty" in the process.

The melancholic is ill in that he stands in a different relationship to his failings than does the mourner. The melancholic does not evidence the shame one would expect of a person who experiences himself as "petty, egoistic, [and] dishonest" (p. 246), and instead demonstrates an "insistent communicativeness which finds satisfaction in self-exposure" (p. 247). Each time Freud returns to the observation of the melancholic's diminished self-regard, he makes use of it to illuminate a different aspect of the unconscious "internal work" (p. 245) of melancholia. This time the observation, with its accrued set of meanings, becomes an important underpinning for a new conception of the ego which to this point has only been hinted at:

> the melancholic's disorder affords [a view] of the constitution of the human ego. We see how in . . . [the melancholic] one part of the ego sets itself over against the other, judges it critically, and, as it were, takes it as its object . . . What we are here becoming acquainted with is the agency commonly called "conscience" . . . and we shall come upon evidence to show that it can become diseased on its own account.
>
> (p. 247)

Here, Freud is re-conceiving the ego in several important ways. These revisions taken together constitute the first of a set of tenets underlying Freud's emerging psychoanalytic theory of unconscious internal object relations: first, the ego, now a psychic structure with conscious and unconscious components ("parts"), can be split; second, an unconscious split-off aspect of the ego has the capacity to generate thoughts and feelings independently – in the case of the critical agency these thoughts and feelings are of a self-observing moralistic, judgmental sort; third, a split-off part of the ego may enter into an unconscious relationship to another part of the ego; and, fourth, a split-off aspect of the ego may be either healthy or pathological.

II

The paper becomes positively fugue-like in its structure as Freud takes up still again – yet in a new way – the sole symptomatic difference between mourning and melancholia:

> If one listens patiently to a melancholic's many and various self-accusations, one cannot in the end avoid the impression that often the most violent of

them are hardly at all applicable to the patient himself, but that with insignificant modifications they do fit someone else, someone whom the patient loves or has loved or should love . . . So we find the key to the clinical picture: we perceive that the self-reproaches are reproaches against a loved object which have been shifted away from it on to the patient's own ego.

(p. 248)

Thus, Freud, as if developing enhanced observational acuity as he writes, sees something he previously had not noticed – that the accusations the melancholic heaps upon himself represent unconsciously displaced attacks on the loved object. This observation serves as a starting point from which Freud goes on to posit a second set of elements of his object relations theory.

In considering the melancholic's unconscious reproaches of the loved object, Freud picks up a thread that he had introduced earlier in the discussion. Melancholia often involves a psychological struggle involving ambivalent feelings for the loved object as "in the case of a betrothed girl who has been jilted" (p. 245). Freud elaborates on the role of ambivalence in melancholia by observing that melancholics show not the slightest humility despite their insistence on their own worthlessness "and always seem as though they felt slighted and had been treated with great injustice" (p. 248). Their intense sense of entitlement and injustice "is possible only because the reactions expressed in their behaviour still proceed from a mental constellation of revolt, which has then, by a certain process, passed over into the crushed state of melancholia" (p. 248).

It seems to me that Freud is suggesting that the melancholic experiences outrage (as opposed to anger of other sorts) at the object for disappointing him and doing him a "great injustice." This emotional protest/revolt is crushed in melancholia as a consequence of "a certain process." It is the delineation of that "certain process" in theoretical terms that will occupy much of the remainder of "Mourning and melancholia."

The reader can hear unmistakable excitement in Freud's voice in the sentence that follows: "There is no difficulty in reconstructing this [transformative] process" (p. 248). Ideas are falling into place. A certain clarity is emerging from the tangle of seemingly contradictory observations, for example, the melancholic's combination of severe self-condemnation and vociferous self-righteous outrage. In spelling out the psychological process mediating the melancholic's movement from revolt (against injustices he has suffered) to a crushed state, Freud, with extraordinary dexterity, presents a radically new conception of the structure of the unconscious:

An object-choice, an attachment of the libido to a particular person, had at one time existed [for the melancholic]; then, owing to a real slight or disappointment coming from this loved person, the object-relationship was shattered. The result was not the normal one of a withdrawal of the libido [loving emotional energy] from this object and a displacement of it on to a new one . . . [Instead,] the object-cathexis [the emotional investment in the object] proved to have little power of resistance [little capacity to maintain the tie to the object], and was brought to an end. But the free libido was not displaced on to another object; it was withdrawn into the ego. There, . . . it [the loving emotional investment which has been withdrawn from the object] . . . served to establish an *identification* of [a part of] the ego with the abandoned object. Thus the shadow of the object fell upon [a part of] the ego, and the latter could henceforth be judged by a special agency [another part of the ego], as though it were an object, the forsaken object. In this way an object-loss was transformed into an ego-loss [a diminution of one's self-regard] and the conflict between the ego and the loved person [was transformed] into a cleavage between the critical activity of [a part of] the ego [later to be called the superego] and [another part of] the ego as altered by identification.

(pp. 248–249)

These sentences represent a powerfully succinct demonstration of the way Freud in this paper was beginning to write/think theoretically and clinically in terms of relationships between unconscious, paired, split-off aspects of the ego (i.e., about unconscious internal object relations[7]). Freud, for the first time, is gathering together into a coherent narrative expressed in higher order theoretical terms his newly conceived revised model of the mind.

There is so much going on in this passage that it is difficult to know where to start in discussing it. Freud's use of language seems to me to afford a port of entry into this critical moment in the development of psychoanalytic thought. There is an important shift in the language Freud is using that serves to convey a re-thinking of an important aspect of his conception of melancholia. The words "object-loss," "lost object," and even "lost as an object of love," are, without comment on Freud's part, replaced by the words "abandoned object" and "forsaken object."

The melancholic's "abandonment" of the object (as opposed to the mourner's loss of the object) involves a paradoxical psychological event: the abandoned object, for the melancholic, is preserved in the form of an identification with it: "Thus [in identifying with the object] the shadow of the object fell upon the ego . . ." (p. 249). In melancholia, the ego is altered not by the glow of the object, but (more darkly) by "the shadow of the object." The shadow metaphor suggests that the melancholic's experience of identifying with the abandoned object has a thin, two-dimensional quality as opposed to a lively, robust feeling tone. The painful experience of loss is short-circuited by the melancholic's identification with the object, thus denying the separateness of the object: the object is me and I am the object. There is no loss; an external object (the abandoned object)

33

is omnipotently replaced by an internal one (the ego-identified-with-the-object).

So, in response to the pain of loss, the ego is twice split forming an internal object relationship in which one split-off part of the ego (the critical agency) angrily (with outrage) turns on another split-off part of the ego (the ego-identified-with-the-object). Although Freud does not speak in these terms, it could be said that the internal object relationship is created for purposes of evading the painful feeling of object-loss. This avoidance is achieved by means of an unconscious "deal with the devil": in exchange for the evasion of the pain of object-loss, the melancholic is doomed to experience the sense of lifelessness that comes as a consequence of disconnecting oneself from large portions of external reality. In this sense, the melancholic forfeits a substantial part of his own life – the three-dimensional emotional life lived in the world of real external objects. The internal world of the melancholic is powerfully shaped by the wish to hold captive the object in the form of an imaginary substitute for it – the ego-identified-with-the-object. In a sense, the internalization of the object renders the object forever captive to the melancholic and at the same time renders the melancholic endlessly captive to it.

A dream of one of my patients comes to mind as a particularly poignant expression of the frozen quality of the melancholic's unconscious internal object world. The patient, Mr K, began analysis a year after the death of his wife of twenty-two years. In a dream that Mr K reported several years into the analysis, he was attending a gathering in which a tribute was to be paid to someone whose identity was unclear to him. Just as the proceedings were getting under way, a man in the audience rose to his feet and spoke glowingly of Mr K's fine character and important accomplishments. When the man finished, the patient stood and expressed his gratitude for the high praise, but said that the purpose of the meeting was to pay tribute to the guest of honor, so the group's attention should be directed to him. Immediately upon Mr K's sitting down, another person stood and again praised the patient at great length. Mr K again stood and after briefly repeating his statement of gratitude for the adulation, he re-directed the attention of the gathering to the honored guest. This sequence was repeated again and again until the patient had the terrifying realization (in the dream) that this sequence would go on forever. Mr K awoke from the dream with his heart racing in a state of panic.

The patient had told me in the sessions preceding the dream that he had become increasingly despairing of ever being able to love another woman and "resume life." He said he has never ceased expecting his wife to return home after work each evening at six-thirty. He added that every family event after her death has been for him nothing more than another occasion at which his wife is missing. He apologized for his lugubrious, self-pitying tones.

I told Mr K that I thought that the dream captured a sense of the way he feels imprisoned in his inability genuinely to be interested in, much less honor, new experiences with people. In the dream, he, in the form of the guests paying endless homage to him, directed to himself what might have been interest paid to someone outside of himself, someone outside of his internally frozen relationship with his wife. I went on to say that it was striking that the honored guest in the dream was not given a name, much less an identity and human qualities which might have stirred curiosity, puzzlement, anger, jealousy, envy, compassion, love, admiration or any other set of feeling responses to another person. I added that the horror he felt at the end of the dream seemed to reflect his awareness that the static state of self-imprisonment in which he lives is potentially endless. (A good deal of this interpretation referred back to many discussions Mr K and I had had concerning his state of being "stuck" in a world that no longer existed.) Mr K responded by telling me that as I was speaking he remembered another part of the dream made up of a single still image of himself wrapped in heavy chains unable to move even a single muscle of his body. He said he felt repelled by the extreme passivity of the image.

The dreams and the discussion that followed represented something of a turning point in the analysis. The patient's response to separations from me between sessions and during weekend and holiday breaks became less frighteningly bleak for him. In the period following this session, Mr K found that he sometimes could go for hours without experiencing the heavy bodily sensation in his chest that he had lived with unremittingly since his wife's death.

While the idea of the melancholic's unconscious identification with the lost/abandoned object for Freud held "the key to the clinical picture" (p. 248) of melancholia, Freud believed that the key to the theoretical problem of melancholia would have to satisfactorily resolve an important contradiction:

> On the one hand, a strong fixation [an intense, yet static emotional tie] to the loved object must have been present; on the other hand, in contradiction to this, the object-cathexis must have had little power of resistance [i.e., little power to maintain that tie to the object in the face of actual or feared death of the object or object-loss as a consequence of disappointment].
>
> (p. 249)

The "key" to a psychoanalytic theory of melancholia that resolves the contradiction of the coexisting strong fixation to the object and the lack of tenacity of that object-tie, lies, for Freud, in the concept of narcissism: "this contradiction seems to imply that the object-choice has been effected on a narcissistic basis, so that the object-cathexis, when obstacles come in its way, can regress to narcissism" (p. 249).

Freud's theory of narcissism, which he had introduced only months earlier in his paper, "On narcissism: an introduction" (1914b), provided an important part of the context for the object relations theory of melancholia that Freud was developing in "Mourning and melancholia." In his narcissism paper, Freud proposed that the normal infant begins in a state of "original" or "primary narcissism" (p. 75), a state in which all emotional energy is ego libido, a form of emotional investment that takes the ego (oneself) as its sole object. The infant makes a step toward the world outside of himself in the form of narcissistic identification – a type of object tie that treats the external object as an extension of oneself.

From the psychological position of narcissistic identification, the healthy infant, in time, develops sufficient psychological stability to engage in a narcissistic form of relatedness to objects in which the tie to the object is largely comprised of a displacement of ego libido from the ego onto the object (Freud, 1914b).

> Thus we form the idea of there being an original libidinal cathexis of the ego, from which some [of the emotional investment in the ego] is later given off to objects, but [the emotional investment in the ego] . . . fundamentally persists and is related to the [narcissistic] object-cathexes, much as the body of an amoeba is related to the pseudopodia which it puts out.
>
> (1914b, p. 75)

In other words, a narcissistic object-tie is one in which the object is invested with emotional energy that originally was directed at oneself (and, in that sense, the object is a stand-in for the self). The movement from narcissistic identification to narcissistic object tie is a matter of a small, but significant shift in the degree of recognition of, and emotional investment in, the otherness of the object.[8]

The healthy infant is able to achieve a differentiation and complementarity between ego-libido and object-libido. In this process of differentiation, he is beginning to engage in a form of object love that is not simply a displacement of love of oneself onto the object. Instead, a more mature form of object love evolves in which the infant achieves relatedness to objects that are experienced as external to himself – outside the realm of the infant's omnipotence.

Herein lies for Freud the key to the theoretical problem – the "contradiction" – posed by melancholia: melancholia is a disease of narcissism. A necessary "preconditions" (1914b, p. 249) for melancholia is a disturbance in early narcissistic development. The melancholic patient in infancy and childhood was unable to move successfully from narcissism to object-love. Consequently, in the face of object loss or disappointment, the melancholic is incapable of mourning, i.e., unable to face the reality of the loss of the object, and, over time, to enter into mature object love with another person. The melancholic does not have the capacity to disengage from the lost object and instead evades the pain of loss through regression from narcissistic object relatedness to narcissistic identification: "the result of which is that in spite of the conflict [disappointment leading to outrage] with the loved person, the love relation need not be given up" (p. 249). As Freud put it in a summary statement near the end of the paper, "So by taking flight into the ego [by means of a powerful narcissistic identification] love escapes extinction" (p. 257).

A misreading of "Mourning and melancholia," to my mind, has become entrenched in what is commonly held to be Freud's view of melancholia (see for example, Gay, 1988, pp. 372–373). What I am referring to is the misconception that melancholia, according to Freud, involves an identification with the hated aspect of an ambivalently loved object that has been lost. Such a reading, while accurate so far as it goes, misses the central point of Freud's thesis. What differentiates the melancholic from the mourner is the fact that the melancholic all along has been able to engage only in narcissistic forms of object relatedness. The narcissistic nature of the melancholic's personality renders him incapable of maintaining a firm connection with the painful reality of the irrevocable loss of the object which is necessary for mourning. Melancholia involves ready, reflexive recourse to regression to narcissistic identification as a way of not experiencing the hard edge of recognition of one's inability to undo the fact of the loss of the object.

Object relations theory, as it is taking shape in the course of Freud's writing this paper, now includes an early developmental axis. The world of unconscious internal object relations is being viewed by Freud as a defensive regression to very early forms of object relatedness in response to psychological pain – in the case of the melancholic, the pain is the pain of loss. The individual replaces what might have become a three-dimensional relatedness to the mortal and at times disappointing external object with a two-dimensional (shadow-like) relationship to an internal object that exists in a psychological domain outside of time (and consequently sheltered from the reality of death). In so doing, the melancholic evades the pain of loss, and, by extension, other forms of psychological pain, but does so at an enormous cost – the loss of a good deal of his own (emotional) vitality.

III

Having hypothesized the melancholic's substitution of an unconscious internal object relationship for an external one and having wed this to a conception of defensive regression to narcissistic identification, Freud turns to a third defining feature of melancholia which, as will be seen, provides the basis for another important feature of his psychoanalytic theory of unconscious internal object relationships:

> In melancholia, the occasions which give rise to the illness extend for the most part beyond the clear case of a loss by death, and include all those situations of being slighted, neglected or disappointed, which can import

opposed feelings of love and hate into the relationship or reinforce an already existing ambivalence. . . . The melancholic's erotic cathexis [erotic emotional investment in the object] . . . has thus undergone a double vicissitude: part of it has regressed to [narcissistic] identification, but the other part, under the influence of the conflict due to ambivalence, has been carried back to the stage of sadism . . .

(1917b, pp. 251–252)

Sadism is a form of object tie in which hate (the melancholic's outrage at the object) becomes inextricably intertwined with erotic love, and in this combined state can be an even more powerful binding force (in a suffocating, subjugating, tyrannizing way) than the ties of love alone. The sadism in melancholia (generated in response to the loss of or disappointment by a loved object) gives rise to a special form of torment for both the subject and the object – that particular mixture of love and hate encountered in stalking. In this sense, the sadistic aspect of the relationship of the critical agency to the split-off ego-identified-with-the-object might be thought of as a relentless, crazed stalking of one split-off aspect of the ego by another – what Fairbairn (1944) would later view as the love/hate bond between the libidinal ego and the exciting object.

This conception of the enormous binding force of combined love and hate is an integral part of the psychoanalytic understanding of the astounding durability of pathological internal object relations. Such allegiance to the bad (hated and hating) internal object is often the source for both the stability of the pathological structure of the patient's personality organization, and for some of the most intractable transference–countertransference impasses that we encounter in analytic work. In addition, the bonds of love mixed with hate account for such forms of pathological relationships as the ferocious ties of the abused child and the battered spouse to their abusers (and the tie of the abusers to the abused). The abuse is unconsciously experienced by both abused and abuser as loving hate and hateful love – both of which are far preferable to no object relationship at all (Fairbairn, 1944).

IV

Employing one of his favorite extended metaphors – the analyst as detective – Freud creates in his writing a sense of adventure, risk-taking and even suspense as he takes on "the most remarkable characteristic of melancholia . . . its tendency to change round into mania – a state which is the opposite of it in its symptoms" (p. 253). Freud's use of language in his discussion of mania – which is inseparable from the ideas he presents – creates for the reader a sense of the fundamental differences between mourning and melancholia, and between healthy (internal and external) object relationships and pathological ones.

I cannot promise that this attempt [to explain mania] will prove entirely satisfactory. It hardly carries us much beyond the possibility of taking one's initial bearings. We have two things to go upon: the first is a psycho-analytic impression, and the second what we may perhaps call a matter of general economic experience. The [psychoanalytic] impression . . . [is] that both disorders [mania and melancholia] are wrestling with the same [unconscious] 'complex', but that probably in melancholia the ego has succumbed to the complex [in the form of a painful feeling of having been crushed] whereas in mania it has mastered it [the pain of loss] or pushed it aside.

(1917b, pp. 253–254)

The second of the two things "we have . . . to go upon" is "general economic experience." In attempting to account for the feelings of exuberance and triumph in mania, Freud hypothesized that the economics of mania – the quantitative distribution and play of psychological forces – may be similar to those seen when

some poor wretch, by winning a large sum of money, is suddenly relieved from chronic worry about his daily bread, or when a long and arduous struggle is finally crowned with success, or when a man finds himself in a position to throw off at a single blow some oppressive compulsion, some false position which he has long had to keep up, and so on.

(1917b, p. 254)

Beginning with the pun on "economic conditions" in the description of the poor wretch who wins a great deal of money, the sentence goes on to capture something of the feel of mania in its succession of images which are unlike any other set of images in the article. These dramatic cameos suggest to me Freud's own understandable magical wishes to have his own "arduous struggle . . . finally crowned with success" or to be able "to throw off at a single blow [his own] . . . oppressive compulsion" to write prodigious numbers of books and articles in his efforts to attain for himself and psychoanalysis the stature they deserve. And like the inevitable end of the expanding bubble of mania, the driving force of the succession of images seems to collapse into the sentences that immediately follow:

This explanation [of mania by analogy to other forms of sudden release from pain] certainly sounds plausible, but in the first place it is too indefinite, and, secondly, it gives rise to more new problems and doubts than we can answer. We will not evade a discussion of them, even though we cannot expect it to lead us to a clear understanding.

(1917b, p. 255)

Freud – whether or not he was aware of it – is doing more than alerting the reader to his uncertainties regarding how to understand mania and its relation to melancholia; he is showing the reader in his use of language, in the structure of his thinking and writing, what it sounds like and feels like to think and write in a way that does not attempt to confuse what is omnipotently, self-deceptively, wished for with what is real; words are used in an effort to simply, accurately, clearly give ideas and situations their proper names.

Bion's work provides a useful context for understanding more fully the significance of Freud's comment that he will not "evade" the new problems and doubts to which his hypothesis gives rise. Bion (1962a) uses the idea of evasion to refer to what he believes to be a hallmark of psychosis: eluding pain rather than attempting to symbolize it for oneself (for example, in dreaming), live with it, and do genuine psychological work with it over time. The latter response to pain – living with it, symbolizing it for oneself, and doing psychological work with it – lies at the heart of the experience of mourning. In contrast, the manic patient who "master[s] the [pain of loss] . . . or push[es] it aside" (Freud, 1917b, p. 254) transforms what might become a feeling of terrible disappointment, aloneness and impotent rage into a state resembling "joy, exultation or triumph" (p. 254).

I believe that Freud here, without explicit acknowledgment – and perhaps without conscious awareness – begins to address the psychotic edge of mania and melancholia. The psychotic aspect of both mania and melancholia involves the evasion of grief as well as a good deal of external reality. This is effected by means of multiple splittings of the ego in conjunction with the creation of a timeless imaginary internal object relationship which omnipotently substitutes for the loss of a real external object relationship. More broadly speaking, a fantasied unconscious internal object world replaces an actual external one, omnipotence replaces helplessness, immortality substitutes for the uncompromising realities of the passage of time and of death, triumph replaces despair, contempt substitutes for love.

Thus Freud (in part explicitly, in part implicitly, and perhaps in part un-knowingly) through his discussion of mania adds another important element to his evolving object relations theory. The reader can hear in Freud's use of language (for example, in his comments on the manic patient's triumphantly pushing aside the pain of loss and exulting in his imaginary victory over the lost object) the idea that the unconscious internal object world of the manic patient is constructed for the purpose of evading, "taking flight" (p. 257) from, the external reality of loss and death. This act of taking flight from external reality has the effect of plunging the patient into a sphere of omnipotent thinking cut off from life lived in relation to actual external objects. The world of external object relations becomes depleted as a consequence of its having been dis-connected from the individual's unconscious internal object world. The patient's experience in the world of external objects is disconnected from the enlivening "fire" (Loewald, 1978, p. 189) of the unconscious internal object world. Conversely, the unconscious internal object world, having been cut off from the world of external objects, cannot grow, cannot "learn from experience" (Bion, 1962a), and cannot enter (in more than a very limited way) into generative "conversations" between unconscious and preconscious aspects of oneself "at the frontier of dreaming" (Ogden, 2001a).

V

Freud concludes the paper with a series of thoughts on a wide range of topics related to mourning and melancholia. Of these, Freud's expansion of the concept of ambivalence is, I believe, the one that represents the most important contribution both to the understanding of melancholia and to the development of his object relations theory. Freud had discussed on many previous occasions, beginning as early as 1900, a view of ambivalence as an unconscious conflict of love and hate in which the individual unconsciously loves the same person he hates, for example, in the distressing ambivalence of healthy Oedipal experience or in the paralyzing torments of the ambivalence of the obsessional neurotic. In "Mourning and melancholia," Freud uses the term "ambivalence" in a strikingly different way; he uses it to refer to a struggle between the wish to live with the living and the wish to be at one with the dead:

> hate and love contend with each other [in melancholia]; the one seeks to detach the libido from the object [thus allowing the subject to live and the object to die], the other to maintain this position of the libido [which is bonded to the immortal internal version of the object].
>
> (1917b, p. 256)

Thus, the melancholic experiences a conflict between, on the one hand, the wish to be alive with the pain of irreversible loss and the reality of death, and on the other hand, the wish to deaden himself to the pain of loss and the knowledge of death. The individual capable of mourning succeeds in freeing himself from the struggle between life and death that freezes the melancholic: "mourning impels the ego to give up the object by declaring the object to be dead and offering the ego the inducement of continuing to live . . ." (p. 257). So the mourner's painful acceptance of the reality of the death of the object is achieved in part because the mourner knows (unconsciously and at times consciously) that his own life, his own capacity for "continuing to live" is at stake.

I am reminded of a patient who began analysis with me almost twenty years after the death of her husband. Ms G told me that not long after her husband's death, she had spent a weekend alone at a lake where for each of the fifteen years before his death, she and her husband had rented a cabin. She told me that during a trip to the lake soon after his death, she had set out alone in a motor-boat and headed toward a labyrinth of small islands and tortuous waterways that she and her husband had explored many times. Ms G said that the idea had come to her with a sense of absolute certainty that her husband was in that set of waterways, and that if she were to have entered that part of the lake, she never would have come out because she would not have been able to "tear" herself away from him. She told me that she had had to fight with all her might not to go to be with her husband.

That decision not to follow her husband into death became an important symbol in the analysis of the patient's choosing to live her life in a world filled with the pain of grief and her living memories of her husband. As the ana-lysis proceeded, that same event at the lake came to symbolize something quite different: the incompleteness of her act of "tearing" herself away from her husband after his death. It became increasingly clear in the transference–countertransference that, in an important sense, a part of herself had gone with her husband into death, that is, an aspect of herself had been deadened and that that had been "alright" with her until that juncture in the analysis.

In the course of the subsequent year of analysis, Ms G experienced a sense of enormous loss – not only the loss of her husband, but also the loss of her own life. She confronted for the first time the pain and sadness of the recognition of the ways she had for decades unconsciously limited herself with regard to utilizing her intelligence and artistic talents as well as her capacities to fully be alive in her everyday experience (including her analysis). (I do not view Ms G as having been manic, or even as having relied heavily on manic defenses, but I believe that she held in common with the manic patient a form of ambivalence that involves a tension between, on the one hand, the wish to live life among the living – internally and externally – and, on the other hand, the wish to exist with the dead in a timeless dead and deadening internal object world.)

Returning to Freud's discussion of mania, the manic patient is engaged in a "struggle of ambivalence [in a desperate unconscious effort to come to life through] loosen[ing] the fixation of the libido to the [internal] object by disparaging it, denigrating it and even as it were killing it" (p. 257).[9] This sentence is surprising: mania represents not only the patient's effort to evade the pain of grief by disparaging and denigrating the object. Mania also represents the patient's (often unsuccessful) attempts *to achieve grief* by freeing himself from the mutual captivity involved in the unconscious internal relationship with the lost object. In order to grieve the loss of the object, one must first kill it, that is, one must do the psychological work of allowing the object to be irrevocably dead, both in one's own mind and in the external world.

By introducing the notion of a form of ambivalence involving the struggle between the wish to go on living and the wish to deaden oneself in an effort to be with the dead, Freud added a critical dimension to his object relations theory: the notion that unconscious internal object relations may have either a

42

living and enlivening quality or a dead and deadening quality (and by extension, every possible combination of the two). Such a way of conceiving the internal object world has been central to recent developments in psychoanalytic theory pioneered by Winnicott (1971a) and Green (1983). These authors have placed emphasis on the importance of the analyst's and the patient's experiences of the aliveness and deadness of the patient's internal object world. The sense of aliveness and deadness of the transference–countertransference is, to my mind, perhaps the single most important measure of the status of the analytic process on a moment-to-moment basis (Ogden, 1995, 1997b). The sound of much of current analytic thinking – and I suspect the sound of psychoanalytic thinking yet to come – can be heard in Freud's "Mourning and melancholia," if we know how to listen.

Freud closes the paper with a voice of genuine humility, breaking off his enquiry mid-thought:

> – But here once again, it will be well to call a halt and to postpone any further explanation of mania . . . As we already know, the interdependence of the complicated problems of the mind forces us to break off every enquiry before it is completed – till the outcome of some other enquiry can come to its assistance.
>
> (1917b, p. 259)

How better to end a paper on the pain of facing reality and the consequences of attempts to evade it? The solipsistic world of a psychoanalytic theorist who is not firmly grounded in the reality of his lived experience with patients is very similar to the self-imprisoned melancholic who survives in a timeless, deathless (and yet dead and deadening) internal object world.

VI Summary

In presenting a reading of Freud's "Mourning and melancholia," I have examined not only the ideas Freud was introducing but, as important, the way he was thinking/writing in this watershed paper. I have attempted to demonstrate how Freud made use of his exploration of the unconscious work of mourning and of melancholia to propose and explore some of the major tenets of a revised model of the mind (which later would be termed "object relations theory"). The principal tenets of the revised model presented in this 1917 paper include: (1) the idea that the unconscious is organized to a significant degree around stable internal object relations between paired split-off parts of the ego; (2) the notion that psychic pain may be defended against by means of the replacement of an external object relationship by an unconscious, fantasized internal object relationship; (3) the idea that pathological bonds of love mixed with hate are among the strongest ties that bind internal objects to one another in a state of mutual captivity; (4) the notion that the psychopathology of internal object relations often involves the use of omnipotent thinking to a degree that cuts off the dialogue between the unconscious internal object world and the world of actual experience with real external objects; and (5) the idea that ambivalence in relations between unconscious internal objects involves not only the conflict of love and hate, but also the conflict between the wish to continue to be alive in one's object relationships and the wish to be at one with one's dead internal objects.

4

On not being able to dream

Much has been written on what dreams mean; relatively little on what it means to dream; and still less on what it means not to be able to dream. What follow are an idea, a story, and an analytic experience, each used as points of entry into the question of what it means – on both a theoretical and an experiential plane – not to be able to dream.

I An idea

Before discussing an idea (more accurately, an inextricably interwoven set of ideas) derived from Bion's work on not being able to dream, a few words regarding Bion's terminology are called for. Bion (1962a) believed that psychoanalytic terminology had become so saturated with "a penumbra of associations" (p. 2) that in order to generate not only fresh ideas, but genuinely new ways of thinking psychoanalytically, it was necessary to introduce a new set of terms, an empty set, that would indicate what is not yet known as opposed to what we imagine we already know. For the purposes of the present discussion, only a small part of this terminology need be defined – if the word "defined" can ever be used with regard to Bion's elusive, evocative, always evolving thinking and writing. Bion (1962a) introduced the term "alpha-function" to refer to the as yet unknown set of mental operations which together transform raw sense impressions ("beta-elements") into elements of experience (termed "alpha-elements") which can be stored as unconscious memory in a form that makes them accessible for creating linkages necessary for unconscious as well as preconscious and conscious psychological work such as dreaming, thinking, repressing, remembering, forgetting, mourning, reverie, and learning from experience.

Beta-elements cannot be linked with one another in the creation of meaning. They might very roughly be compared with "snow" on a malfunctioning television screen in which no single visual scintillation or group of scintillations can be linked with other scintillations to form an image or even a meaningful pattern. Beta-elements (in the absence of alpha-function to convert them to alpha-elements) are fit only for evacuation or for storage – not as memory – but as psychic noise. (The "snow" and "noise" metaphors are my own and represent interpretations of Bion.)

In *Learning from Experience*, Bion (1962a) introduced a radically new set of ideas regarding what is involved both in dreaming and in not being able to dream.[1]

> An emotional experience occurring in sleep . . . does not differ from the emotional experience occurring during waking life in that the perceptions of the emotional experience have in both instances to be worked upon by alpha-function before they can be used for dream thoughts . . .

> If the patient cannot transform his [raw sensory] emotional experience into alpha-elements, he cannot dream. Alpha-function transforms sense impressions into alpha-elements which resemble, and may in fact be identical with, the visual images with which we are familiar in dreams, namely, the elements that Freud regards as yielding their latent content [when interpreted in analysis or self-analysis] . . . Failure of alpha-function means that the patient cannot dream and therefore cannot sleep. [In as much as] alpha-function makes the [raw] sense impressions . . . available for conscious [thought] and dream-thought the patient who cannot dream cannot go to sleep and cannot wake up. Hence the peculiar condition seen clinically when a psychotic patient behaves as if he were in precisely this state.
>
> (pp. 6–7)

In the space of these two dense paragraphs, Bion offers a reconceptualization of the role of dreaming in human life. Dreaming occurs continuously day and night though we are aware of it in waking states only in derivative form, for example, in reverie states occurring in an analytic session (see Ogden, 1997a, 1997b, 2001a). If a person is unable to transform raw sensory data into unconscious elements of experience that can be stored and made accessible for linking, he is incapable of dreaming (which involves making emotional linkages in the creation of dream-thoughts).[2]

Instead of having a dream (experienced as a dream), the individual incapable of alpha-function registers only raw sensory data. For such a person, the raw sensory data (beta-elements) experienced in sleep are indistinguishable from those occurring in waking life.[3] Unable to differentiate waking and sleeping states, the patient "cannot go to sleep and cannot wake up" (Bion, 1962a, p. 7). Such states are regularly observed in psychotic patients who do not know if they are awake or dreaming because what might have become a dream (were the patient capable of alpha-function) becomes, instead, an hallucination in sleep or waking life. Hallucinations are the opposite of dreaming and of unconscious thinking in a waking state.

Conversely, not all psychic events occurring in sleep (even those events in visual imagistic form that we remember on waking) merit the name "dream." Psychological events occurring in sleep that appear to be dreams, but are not dreams include "dreams" to which no associations can be made, hallucinations in sleep, the repetitive (unchanging) "dreams" of those suffering from traumatic neuroses, imageless "dreaming" consisting only of an intense feeling state or a muscular action in sleep. Though these phenomena occurring in sleep may appear to be dreams, they involve no unconscious psychological work – the work of dreaming – which results in psychological growth. One can hallucinate for a lifetime without the slightest bit of psychological work getting done. For Bion, as I understand him, dreaming – if it is to merit the name – must involve unconscious psychological work achieved through the linking of elements of experience (which have been stored as memory) in the creation of dream-thought. This work of making unconscious linkages – as opposed to forms of psychic evacuation such as hallucination, excessive projective identification, manic defense, and paranoid delusion – allows one unconsciously and consciously to think about and make psychological use of experience. A person unable to learn from (make use of) experience is imprisoned in the hell of an endless, unchanging world of what is.

Bion goes on to flesh out his revision of the analytic conception of dreaming:

> A man talking to a friend converts the sense impressions of this emotional experience into alpha-elements, thus becoming capable of dream-thoughts and therefore of undisturbed consciousness of the facts whether the facts are the events in which he participates or his feelings about those events or both. He is able to remain "asleep" or unconscious of certain elements that cannot penetrate the barrier presented by his "dream". Thanks to the "dream" he can continue uninterruptedly to be awake, that is, awake to the fact that he is talking to his friend, but asleep to elements which, if they could penetrate the barrier of his "dreams", would lead to domination of his mind by what are ordinarily unconscious ideas and emotions.

> The dream [which in health is continuously being generated unconsciously] makes a barrier against mental phenomena which might overwhelm the patient's awareness that he is talking to a friend, and, at the same time, makes it impossible for awareness that he is talking to a friend to overwhelm his phantasies.
>
> (1962a, p. 15)

Here, Bion expands his conception of dreaming in such a way that the role of dreaming is no longer limited to constructing narratives (with manifest and latent meanings) by means of linking stored elements of experience

47

(alpha-elements). Bion in this passage reverses the conventional wisdom that the ability to fall asleep is a pre-condition for dreaming. He proposes instead that dreaming is what makes it possible to fall asleep and to wake up. Dreaming, as it is being newly conceived, *creates* consciousness and unconsciousness and maintains the difference between the two. The term "being asleep" becomes in Bion's hands a conception of being "unconscious of certain elements [the repressed] that cannot penetrate the barrier presented by his 'dream'" (p. 15). And similarly, being awake is now synonymous with being uninterruptedly conscious of what is going on in waking life (for example, listening to a patient, reading a book, viewing a film). This is achieved by means of waking unconscious dreaming. Both forms of dreaming – that done in sleep and in waking unconscious dreaming – generate a living semi-permeable barrier separating and connecting conscious and unconscious life. In the absence of waking unconscious dreaming, not only would consciousness be over-run by repressed unconscious thoughts and feelings; in addition, actual experience in the realm of external reality would be unavailable to the individual for purposes of unconscious psychological work. Without undisturbed access to external reality, one has no lived experience to work on or work with.

Dreaming, from this vantage point, is what allows us to create and maintain the structure of our mind organized around the differentiation of, and the mediated conversation between, our conscious life and our unconscious life. If a person is unable to dream, he is unable to differentiate between unconscious psychic constructions (e.g., dreams) and waking perceptions, and consequently is unable to go to sleep and unable to wake up. The two states are indistinguishable and in such instances the person is psychotic. Bion observes that the psychotic's inability to discriminate conscious and unconscious experience results in a "peculiar lack of 'resonance'" (p. 15) in his "rational thoughts," reported dreams, facial expressions, speech patterns, and so on:

> What he [the psychotic] says clearly and in articulated speech is one-dimensional. It has no overtones or undertones of meaning. It makes the listener inclined to say "so what?" It has no capacity to evoke a train of thought.
>
> (pp. 15–16)

The differentiation of, and interplay between, unconscious and conscious life is created by – not simply reflected in – dreaming. In this important sense, dreaming makes us human. The essence of Bion's "idea" – his conception of not being able to dream – is conveyed in an allegory that could have been written by no psychoanalyst other than Bion:

> It used once to be said that a man had a nightmare because he had indigestion and that is why he woke up in a panic. My version is: The sleeping patient is

48

panicked; because he cannot have a nightmare he cannot wake up or go to sleep; he has had mental indigestion ever since.

(p. 8)

The mental "indigestion" to which Bion is metaphorically referring is the experience of being timelessly ("ever since") interred in a world of undreamable (indigestible) panic – a form of panic unavailable for dreaming and other forms of unconscious psychological work, a panic one can neither remember nor forget, neither hold secret nor communicate. It is a panic one can only evacuate (for example, as in hallucination, delusion or massive projective identification) or annihilate (through fragmentation or suicide).

Bion's allegory has the feel of a myth because of the universal truth it manages to convey in the simplest of everyday words and images.

II A story

It is fascinating to read Borges' (1941a) fiction, "Funes the memorious," while holding in mind Bion's conception of the role of dreaming in the structuring of the mind and his view of the consequences of not being able to dream. "Funes the memorious" was written more than twenty years prior to the publication of *Learning from Experience*. Despite this accident of time, to my mind, no literary work has succeeded as well as Borges' "Funes" in bringing to life in the medium of language the experience of not being able to dream and consequently not being able to go to sleep or to wake up.

I am not presenting Borges' fiction as psychoanalytic data or as evidence supporting the value or verity of Bion's ideas. I *am* inviting the reader to experience some of the pleasure to be had in marveling at, playing with, and adding his or her own voice to the imaginary conversation between Bion and Borges on the subject of not being able to dream.

"Funes the Memorious" begins:

I remember him (I have no right to utter this sacred verb, only one man on earth had that right and he is dead) with a dark passion flower in his hand, seeing it as no one has ever seen it, though he might look at it from the twilight of dawn till that of evening, a whole lifetime.

(1941a, p. 59)

This remarkably beautiful, enigmatic opening sentence and those that immediately follow create an intoning, almost reverential sound and rhythm as the words "I remember" echo down the page: "I remember him," "I remember him," "I remember (I think)," "I remember," "I clearly remember."

As the story unfolds, Borges (the character and speaker who cannot be clearly differentiated from Borges, the author) tells the reader that his memory of his first encounter with Funes is an image of a boy running with "almost secret footsteps" (p. 60). The phrase "almost secret" is a wonderfully compact way of conveying how virtually every experience – whether a waking perception, a memory or a dream – has the quality of something hidden (held secret) by what is perceived and of something revealed by what is hidden (in being *almost* secret).

Ireneo Funes, who seems always to be running, is a momentary presence with a "cigarette in his hard face" and a "shrill, mocking" voice. Borges is told that Funes, who assiduously avoids contact with people, has the ability, "without consulting the sky" (p. 60), to always know the time precisely – "like a clock" (p. 60). The "chronometrical" (p. 61) Funes is presented as no ordinary boy: he has a bizarre, slightly menacing, not fully human quality.

Three years later, on returning to the town where he first encountered Funes, Borges is told that the boy had been thrown from a horse and is "hopelessly paralyzed":

> I remember the sensation of uneasy magic the news produced in me . . . [Hearing the news] had much of the quality of a dream made up of previous elements . . . Twice I saw him [lying on his cot] behind the iron grating of the window, which harshly emphasized his condition as a perpetual prisoner . . .
>
> (p. 61)

Funes soon learns that Borges has brought with him ("not without a certain vaingloriousness," Borges admits) three Latin texts as well as a Latin dictionary. Funes dispatches a note to Borges asking to borrow any one of the Latin volumes along with the dictionary (since he knew not a word of Latin). He promises to return them "almost immediately" (everything is instantaneous in the world Funes occupies). Borges arranges to have the books delivered to Funes. A few days later, Borges goes to the house where Funes lives with his mother to retrieve his books before returning to Buenos Aires. In the dim light of evening, Borges makes his way through a series of rooms, passageways, and patios, to find Funes in a back room where "the darkness seemed complete" (p. 62). Even before entering the room, Borges could hear Funes, who, "with morose delight," was speaking "Roman syllables" that were "indecipherable, interminable" (p. 62). Later that night, Borges learned that the syllables Funes had been speaking from memory were taken from the twenty-fourth chapter of the seventh book of Pliny's *Naturalis Historia*:

> The subject of that chapter is memory; the last words were *ut nihil non iisdem verbis redderetur auditum* [so that nothing having been heard can be re-told in the same words].
>
> (p. 62)

Despite the touches of humor (for example, the self-parodying, over-done displays of erudition), there is a sense of horror in the sound of the shrill, mocking voice – more a disembodied voice than a person speaking – endlessly reciting Roman syllables (meaningless sounds as opposed to words used as symbols for purposes of communication).

Borges describes some of what occurred during the night he spent with Funes. Ireneo explained that before being thrown by the horse, he had been

> what all humans are: blind, deaf, addlebrained and absent-minded . . . For nineteen years he had lived as one in a dream: he looked without seeing, listened without hearing, forgetting everything, almost everything. When he fell, he became unconscious; when he came to, the present was almost intolerable in its richness and sharpness, as were his most distant and trivial memories. Somewhat later he learned that he was paralyzed. The fact scarcely interested him. He reasoned (he felt) that his immobility was a minimum price to pay. Now his perception and his memory were infallible.
>
> (p. 63)

Funes for nineteen years had lived "as one in a dream," not as a person cyclically waking and sleeping. He had lived as if in a dream from which he could not wake up. It might be said that before the fall, Funes had lived as a figure in a dream without a dreamer or perhaps a figure in his own dream or a figure in someone else's dream. His life – I imagine – was something like that of a bird or other animal in his lack of awareness of the difference between himself and the natural world of which he was a part. Funes did not deduce the time from the position of the sun or the moon in the sky; rather, he experienced the time, he *was* the time, in as much as he was a part of the sun and the moon and the sky and the light and the dark. The wonder lay in the fact he could speak, though his speech was little more than the "communications" of the hourly chimes of a clock or the crow of a rooster at daybreak.

After Funes "came to," he did not return to his previous state. With his newly acquired "infallible" powers of perception and memory, Funes

> knew by heart the forms of the southern clouds at dawn on the 30th of April, 1882, and could compare them in his memory with the mottled streaks of a book in Spanish binding he had only seen once and with the outlines of the foam raised by an oar in the Rio Negro the night before the Quebracho uprising. These memories were not simple ones; each visual image was linked to muscular sensations, thermal sensations, etc.
>
> (pp. 63–64)

Ireneo, in linking the clouds in the southern skies, the streaks on the binding of a book, and the shape of the foam raised by an oar in the Rio Negro, was creating a network of linkages in which each element is connected with every other element, not according to a system of logical or even emotional associations, but by purely sensory linkages (for example, of shape, temperature, kinaesthetic feel, and so on). The result is a massive, sprawling, solipsistic ever-expanding whole.

Funes had invented his own number system in which each number was replaced by a word, for example, "in place of seven thousand fourteen, *The Railroad* . . . In place of five hundred, he would say *nine* . . . I tried to explain to him [in vain] that this rhapsody of incoherent terms was precisely the opposite of a system of numbers" (pp. 64–65).

For Ireneo, perceptions and memories were so precise and so massive in detail that he lost the capacity to organize his perceptions and memories into categories and lost all sense of the continuity of objects over time and space:

> Not only was it difficult for him to comprehend that the generic symbol *dog* embraces so many unlike individuals of diverse size and form; it bothered him that the dog at three fourteen (seen from the side) should have the same name as the dog at three fifteen (seen from the front).
>
> (p. 65)

On "coming to," Funes lived no longer like a figure in a dream; he had become like a dreamer of a "vertiginous world" (p. 65) never before conceived of by anyone. There was a major problem inherent in this feat: He was a prisoner in the psychological world he "dreamed." He could not wake up from his "dreaming" in the sense that he could not think about what he was perceiving. Borges darkly comments later in the story: "I suspect . . . that [Funes] was not very capable of thought. To think is to forget differences, generalize, make abstractions" (p. 66). The world Funes created was meaningless in that relationships among its parts adhered to no system of logic or even of illogic. Funes existed as a dreamer of a meaningless dream that he did not know he was dreaming. Such a "dream" is a dream that is not a genuine dream in Bion's (1962a) sense of the word – it accomplishes no psychological work, it changes nothing and goes nowhere. This type of "dreaming," like an hallucination, makes it impossible to distinguish waking from dreaming, and, consequently, as Bion observed, impossible to go to sleep and to wake up.

Living as one perpetually producing meaningless "dreams," Funes found that it "was [as Bion would have expected] very difficult for him to sleep" (p. 66). Paradoxically, to sleep, for Funes, would have meant to be able to wake up from his self-created (quasi-hallucinatory) world cluttered with infinite details that add up to nothing. To sleep, would have been to wake up from his state of immersion in a sea of unutilizable perceptions and "memories" (akin to Bion's beta-elements) by having a genuine dream that serves to separate conscious from unconscious experience, thus making it possible to wake up (that is, to be able to feel the difference between sleeping and waking, between dreaming and hallucinating).

In his effort to sleep, Funes imagined new houses to the east that he had never seen: "He imagined them to be black, compact, made of homogeneous darkness; in that direction he would turn his face in order to sleep" (p. 66).

To be able to sleep – to dream a dream that generates unconscious dream-thoughts – would have required of Funes an ability he lacked – the capacity to imagine the black houses made of homogeneous darkness and to know that he was imagining (and on waking, to know that he had been asleep and dreaming). For Funes, who could not forget, the only form of imagining that he could be certain he could differentiate from remembering was to imagine what he had never seen. What he "imagined" was "homogenous darkness," the most calming of all states for Funes because it offered a reprieve from an external world that was senselessly teeming and swarming with perceived and remembered details. "Imagining" in this way was as close as Funes could come to genuine dreaming: it was a state of mind in which it was possible for Funes to begin to differentiate the inner and the outer, the invented and the real, the conscious and the unconscious. This psychological state held the possibility for Funes of his being able to go to sleep and wake up. To make matters even more complicated, to wake up would not have been a victory to be celebrated unambivalently by Funes because that to which he would have awoken was a frightening world of fully human people whose presence he could hardly bear. (Borges, the author, too, was a man who for long periods of time suffered from insomnia and found being with other people almost unbearable.)

In order to sleep, Funes "would also imagine himself at the bottom of the river, rocked and annihilated by the current" (p. 66). The implacability of remembered images (*the* river, not an imagined river) is giving way in this sentence first to imageless, rhythmic sensation-sounds ("river, rocked"), and finally to the annihilation of the infallibly perceiving, infinitely remembering mind named Funes. There is an ominous suggestion here that dying (annihilating himself psychically or physically) might be the only form of "sleep" Funes could achieve.

The story closes simply and quietly: "Ireneo Funes died in 1889, of congestion of the lungs" (p. 66).

Funes' death by congestion of the lungs has an uncanny resemblance to the patient in Bion's (1962a) allegory:

> The sleeping patient is panicked; because he cannot have a nightmare he cannot wake up or go to sleep; he has had mental indigestion ever since.
>
> (p. 8)

The opposite of a good dream is not a nightmare but a dream that cannot be dreamt: what might have become a dream remains timelessly suspended in a no-man's land where there is neither imagination nor reality, neither forgetting nor remembering, neither sleeping nor waking up.

III An analytic experience

The third vantage point from which I will address the question of what it means to be unable to dream is an experience with a patient that occurred in the third year of the analysis.

When I went to meet Ms C for our session, on opening the door to the waiting room, I was startled to find her standing only a foot or so in front of me. The effect was disconcerting: my face felt too close to hers. I reflexively averted my gaze.

Once Ms C lay down on the couch, I began by saying to her that something unusual had just happened in the waiting room. She probably had noticed that I had been startled to find her standing closer to me than usual when I opened the waiting room door. Ms C did not respond to my implicit question as to whether she had noticed my surprise. Instead, she rather mechanically delivered what felt to me to be a series of pre-packaged analytic ideas: "Perhaps I was sexualizing or perverting the event. Maybe I was angrily attempting to be 'in your face.'" It seemed that these ideas were, for Ms C, fully inter-changeable. She went on to develop these "thoughts" at length in a way that felt numbing.

In an effort to say something that felt to me less disconnected from feelings involved in the event as I had experienced it, I said to Ms C that I thought she might have been afraid that I would not see her in the waiting room had she not positioned herself as she had. (We had talked previously of her feeling insubstantial and behaving in such a way as to lead people to look through her as if she were not there.) In making the interpretation, I also had in mind the patient's derisive depiction of her parents as "schizoid people" with good intentions, but "no idea" who the patient was and is. But even as I was saying these words, my interpretation felt as vacant as those of Ms C.

The patient agreed with what I said and without pause went on in a manner that was familiar to both of us, to tell me about the myriad events of her day. Ms C spoke rapidly, jumping from topic to topic, each of which concerned a specific aspect of the "organization of her life" (a term she and I used to refer to her operational thinking and behavior). She told me how long she had jogged that morning, whom she had met in the elevator of her apartment building on the way to and from the run, and so on. Early on, I had interpreted both the content and the process – to the extent as I thought I understood them – of such recountings of the seemingly inexhaustible minutiae of her life.

Over the course of time, I had learned that my interpretations were not only without value to Ms C, they were often counter-productive in that they elicited from her an increasingly pressured flow of verbiage. Moreover, it felt to me that often my need to interpret was motivated by a wish to assert the fact that I was present in the room. I was also at times aware retrospectively that my inter-pretations had been, in part, angry efforts to turn back on the patient her seemingly unending torrent of words and psychoanalytic formulations, which I found depleting and suffocating.

In the session under discussion, after talking about her morning's activities, Ms C began speaking about having slept restlessly the previous night. She said that she had awoken four times during the night, each time getting up to get a glass of water and to urinate. As was characteristic of her, she made no reference to her emotional response to any of the events she described. While she was speaking, my mind wandered to another patient, Mr N, with whom I had worked more than fifteen years earlier. That patient had been addicted for several years to a prescription narcotic. I recalled speaking to Mr N the day after he had been hospitalized for injuries he had sustained in a boating accident. In that telephone conversation, Mr N told me that non-stop, twenty-four-hours-a-day, "shopping-center Christmas music" was coming from the wall behind his hospital bed, and that it was driving him crazy. He said that he had repeatedly told the nurses about it, but that they had said they could do nothing to stop it. Mr N, weeks later, recognized the grating music to have been an auditory hallucination resulting from drug withdrawal from the narcotic to which he had been addicted. This reverie about Mr N left me feeling extremely anxious, but the reasons for my uneasiness were opaque to me.

My thoughts then moved to the fact that in Ms C's analysis there had been periods of time when I had found myself disoriented in a way, and to a degree, that I had not experienced with any other patient. There had been a number of instances when I had lost track of the time, not knowing whether we had gone on far past the end of the session or whether we were somewhere in the middle of it. I felt terrible anxiety at these times, feeling that I had no way to figure out where we were in the session. At such moments, I would stare at the face of the clock in my office only to find that it seemed to stare back at me blankly, not helping in the least to relieve my confusion and anxiety. I had experienced these states of mind as deeply disturbing signs that I was losing my mind. Oddly, each time, on regaining my bearings, the experience seemed quite remote and devoid of feelings. (Borges' parenthetical comment about Funes' response to his paralysis captures the essence of that state of detachment: "The fact scarcely interested him.")

Ms C then spoke about her plans to sell the condominium in which she had lived for the previous twelve years and her hopes to buy a house. She talked about how nice it would be to have a separate room that she could use as a study and about her annoyance that her real estate agent was urging her to have her condominium "staged" (outfitted and arranged by an interior decorator in order to increase the appeal and selling price of the condominium). Any part of this account seemingly would have offered ample opportunity for interpretation. For example, I might have linked the demand that her condominium be "staged" to Ms C's feeling that her mother and I could not recognize and accept her as she really is; or I could have connected the repeated cycle of taking in water and emptying her bladder with her long-standing pattern of seeming to take in my interpretations only to evacuate them shortly thereafter. I refrained from making these and many other possible interpretations because I felt that to have done so would have been to join the patient in the use of words to obscure my feeling of the arbitrariness of our happening to be in the same room – a room that did not feel like an analytic consulting room at that moment. I made a conscious effort to orient myself to what I was doing there by recalling Ms C's reasons for having come to see me in the first place: she had felt intense feelings of pointlessness in virtually every sector of her life, particularly in her efforts to develop a love relationship with a man. I recalled her having told me in the initial meeting that she had unsuccessfully tried a variety of anti-depressant medications. My thoughts again turned to my former patient, Mr N and his difficulties with prescribed pain medications.

As I thought more about my having silently concurred with Mr N's "recognition" that his Christmas music hallucination was a neurological symptom that conveyed no utilizable unconscious meaning, it increasingly seemed to me that I had unconsciously colluded with him in evading feelings of sadness. I had foreclosed the possibility that the non-stop shopping center music was not simply a neurological symptom, but a psychologically meaningful creation that had held particular unconscious symbolic meaning for him. It occurred to me (for the first time) that of all the things that he might have hallucinated auditorily, it was the sound of endless, crassly commercialized Christmas music that he had heard. It was the sound of the worst form of mockery, not only of music (which the patient deeply loved), but also of the Christmases before his parents' divorce which had been some of the happiest and most loving family events that Mr N could remember.

My recollections of Mr N's Christmas music hallucination and my emotional responses and associations to it led me to become aware that having a reverie – any reverie – that I could make use of analytically was an extremely rare event in my work with Ms C. It was not that my thoughts had not wandered during earlier sessions with Ms C; what struck me at this point in the session was how little psychological work I had been able to do with my reverie experiences. There was a feeling of relief in this recognition.

Ms C began the next session by telling me a dream[4] that she had had the previous night:

> I'm at a session with you. [Ms C pointed to the floor.] It's here in this office in the morning, at this time. It's this session. Then it seemed to shift and I am in another part of a large office suite. There are lots of rooms, not just the ones that are really here. I looked around. There was stuff all over the place. There were old yellowing plastic plates, empty paint cans – I can't remember what else – books and papers strewn all over the floor. It makes me anxious just to think of it. I couldn't tell what the room was used for. There were also

paintings leaning against the wall five or six deep, but I could see only the back of the outside one. There is a desk drawer that I very badly want to open to see what's inside, but I woke up before I could open it. I was very disappointed that the dream was interrupted before I could look inside the drawer.

Ms C was quiet after telling me the dream, which was significant because any sustained silence was highly unusual for her. I felt as if she were inviting me – by giving me more room than usual – to think and talk (just as there were more rooms in the second part of the dream). I said that the first part of the dream seemed to be an unadorned image of my office as it "really is." Ms C said, "Yes, it did feel flat."

I told her that the second part of the dream felt to me very different from the first: "It is set in a place that is not a real place, but an imaginary one – a much larger place with many more rooms than there really are here." (I was reminded of Ms C's wish to have an extra room in the house she hoped to buy to use for thinking – a study.) She and I talked about the way in which the room at first felt like a mess, cluttered with an enormous number of things and about her feeling of being unable to tell what the function of the room was. I commented on her feeling of disappointment at the end of the dream. Ms C responded by saying that the dream had not left her feeling disappointed. She said that something changed at the end that was hard for her to describe. Ms C talked about the canvasses that were stacked against the wall revealing only the back of the outermost of them, which made her curious about what was painted on the fronts of them. She said, "It was disappointing to awaken from the dream before I was able to see what was in the drawer, but it was a good disappointment – if that makes any sense. It seems strange to say this, but I actually feel excited about what I might dream tonight." Ms C. was silent for several minutes. During that time, I thought about E, a close friend for many years – a man in his 70s – who had died the previous weekend. During that week following his death, I was continually either consciously thinking of him or experiencing a diffuse background feeling of sadness and a sense of someone or something missing. So the fact that I was thinking about him did not distinguish this moment in the session with Ms C from my experience with each of my other patients that day or that week. However, what was unique to that moment in the work with Ms C was the particular way I was feeling about E. With each patient (and within each hour with each patient), the way in which I experienced the loss of E was specific to what was going on at that moment at an unconscious level in the analytic relationship. In the period of silence following the discussion of Ms C's dream, I thought of the previous Saturday evening during which I had spent some time at E's bedside along with his wife and their grown children. E was in a deep coma at that point. I recalled the sense of surprise and relief I felt about how warm E's hands had felt when I held them.

The fact that he had been comatose for almost a day at that point had led me to expect that his body would feel cold.

My thoughts moved from these images and sensations concerning E to the surprise and discomfort I had felt during the encounter with Ms C in the waiting room the previous day. The reverie involving the unexpected warmth in E's hand contributed to my becoming consciously aware of the growing affection I had been feeling for Ms C over the course of the past several weeks. After a time I said to Ms C that I thought I had been off the mark in the previous session when I said that I thought that she had been worried that I would not notice her in the waiting room if she were not standing very close to me when I opened the door. I told her that I now thought that perhaps she simply had wanted to be close to me and I was sorry that I had not allowed myself to know that at the time. Ms C cried. After a little while she thanked me for having understood something that she herself had not known, but which she none-theless felt to be true. She added that it is rare for her to know something in this way without a million other things flying around in her head.

I felt intensely sad at that point in the session which was almost over. It seemed that Ms C, then in her 40s, had missed a good deal of the joys and sorrows of a lived life – as I had missed out on experiencing Ms C's feelings of warmth toward me the previous day in the waiting room (and would miss out on a continuing friendship with E). It was of considerable comfort to me to feel that while Ms C had forever lost many opportunities to be alive, her life was not at an end. She had put this quite beautifully in saying that her disappoint-ment at the end of her dream was not a feeling of despondency but a feeling of excitement about what she might dream that night.

IV Discussion

Ms C's unceasing verbiage – seemingly impervious to interpretation – had engendered in me during the first years of the analysis feelings of helplessness, anger and claustrophobic fear (for example, feelings of being suffocated or of drowning). In the first of the two sessions I have presented, my mind wandered to the Christmas music hallucinations of my former patient, Mr N. These recollections led me to think of the brief periods of countertransference psychosis in my work with Ms C during which I had become lost in relation to time not knowing when we had begun or what time we were to end the session or how far into the session we were. What was most disturbing about this was the feeling that I had no place to turn in my effort to locate myself. The face of the clock felt frighteningly blank.

Only in retrospect was I able to view the moments of countertransference psychosis in the analysis of Ms C as a response to her having flooded me with words (which I had experienced much as Borges described the effect of Funes' onslaught of "Roman syllables" that did not function as meaningful elements of language used for purposes of symbolic communication). Ms C's non-stop verbiage had had the effect of disrupting my capacity to make use of my reverie experience (which is central to my being able to do the psychological work necessary to "catch the drift" [Freud, 1923, p. 239] of what is happening at an unconscious level in the analytic relationship [see Ogden, 1997a, 1997b, 2001a for discussions of my use of reverie experience in analytic work]). In a sense, in the analysis with Ms C, I was experiencing chronic reverie-deprivation[5] which, like sleep deprivation, can precipitate a psychosis. The countertransference psychosis allowed me to experience first-hand something like the patient's psychotic experience of not being able to dream (either while asleep or unconsciously while awake).

I experienced considerable relief on recognizing the degree to which the patient and I had been unable to dream in the analytic setting – including our inability to engage in states of reverie that were utilizable for purposes of communication with ourselves and with one another. The dream Ms C told me at the beginning of the second of these sessions seemed to me a triptych in which the first part of the dream was a flat depiction of the way my office "really is." Like a snapshot, it had the feel of a simple, mechanical registration of what was perceived. I view this part of the dream as a dream that is not a dream, but rather a visual image in sleep that is composed of elements that cannot be linked and upon which no unconscious psychological work can be done. Consequently, it did not give rise to associations in either the patient's mind or my own. Ms C compliantly agreed with my account of it.

The second part of the dream had the feel of a genuine dream both depicting the experience of not being able to dream and doing unconscious psychological work with that experience.[6] The chaotic room was filled with disconnected elements – yellowed plastic plates, empty paint cans, books and papers – a morass of disparate elements not adding up to anything. And yet, as the dream proceeded, the elements were transformed into something that was by no means meaningless: the empty paint cans, for example, later in the dream became linked to paint with which paintings could be made, man-made imaginative images (not yet seen). Even Ms C's "throw-away" comment, "I can't remember what else [was in the room]," reflected the fact that the patient was now able to forget (repress). As Borges (1941a), put it in speaking of Funes, "To think is to [be able to] forget differences, generalize, make abstractions" (p. 66).

The third part of the dream – centering around the patient's intense curiosity about the contents of the unopened desk drawer – seems to me to involve an enlivening tension between what is seen (i.e., what is available to conscious awareness) and what is not (i.e., what is dynamically unconscious). The differentiated, internally communicating mind is filled with possibilities that spark the imagination like the "almost secret footsteps" of Ireneo Funes, and allows for both unconscious and conscious psychological work to be done. For example, Ms C made a thoughtful discrimination in modifying an aspect of my response to the third part of the dream: She emphasized the ascendancy of the feeling of enlivening possibility (as opposed to disappointment) in the ending of the dream and in her feelings on awakening from it.

In the weeks that followed the two sessions I have presented, I became better able to understand something that had continued to trouble me about these meetings. I came to view my anxious withdrawal from Ms C in the waiting room as a manifestation of my inability to dream Ms C's emotional experience (her undreamt dream) which she had evacuated into me. Once I became able to observe the analytic interaction from this vantage point, it became possible for the patient and me to create in the sessions an intrapsychic–interpersonal field in which to "dream" the transference–countertransference and to verbally symbolize our responses to that "dream" in the form of interpretations. The outcome of the psychological work that Ms C and I did in this way included a fuller understanding of the patient's relationship to her (internal object) father. Ms C spoke about her experience of the "loss of her father" during her adolescence. It seemed to her that when she was about twelve, he had abruptly, and completely unexpectedly, closed off the loving relationship that the two of them had enjoyed up to that point "as if it had never happened." Ms C had known in a diffuse way, but had not previously been able to think or articulate for herself, that both she and her father had been frightened by the romantic and sexual feelings he felt toward her and she toward him. She said, "What makes it [the emotional breach] so sad is that it was so unnecessary." These feelings and thoughts were used to do further psychological work with "the waiting room incident": the patient and I became better able to dream (and thereby live) that experience together – an experience which kept changing as we kept dreaming it.

5

What's true and whose idea was it?

The practice of psychoanalysis is, I believe, most fundamentally an effort on the part of analyst and analysand to say something that feels both true to the emotional experience of any given moment of an analytic session and utilizable by the analytic pair for psychological work.

In this chapter I entertain a number of ideas related to the question of what we, as psychoanalysts, mean when we say something is true and what one person's thinking has to do with that of another with regard to what is true. My intention is to begin to explore the paradox that human emotional truths are both universal and exquisitely idiosyncratic to each individual, and are both timeless and highly specific to a given moment of life. As will become apparent, the various questions that I raise spill into one another and, as a result, the discussion often doubles back on itself as I re-think, from another perspective, matters addressed earlier.

Many of the ideas in this chapter are responses to concepts discussed by Bion. I attempt to locate the source of the ideas I present, but it is difficult for me to say with any confidence where Bion's ideas leave off and mine begin. Since the matter of "Whose idea was it?" is at the core of this contribution, it seems only fitting that it be faced in the experience of writing and reading this chapter.

The question of whether an analytic exchange achieves an articulation of something that is true (or at least "relatively truthful," Bion, 1982, p. 8) is not an abstruse theoretical matter best left to philosophers. As analysts, we are at almost every moment of an analytic session asking ourselves and tentatively answering (or, more accurately, responding to) this question. I present a detailed account of an initial analytic meeting in which I illustrate some of the ways I approach both the question of what is emotionally true at specific junctures in the session and the question of who is the author of the idea that is felt to be true.

I Whose idea was it?

In asking, "Whose idea was it?" I am inquiring into what it means for a person to claim, or to have attributed to him or her, original authorship of an idea regarding what is true to human emotional experience and how those ideas serve as an influence on the thinking of others. In reading Freud and Klein, for example, how are we to determine who is to be credited with original author- ship of the concept of an unconscious internal object world. In "Mourning and melancholia," Freud (1917b) introduced what I view as the essential elements of what would later be termed by Fairbairn (1952) "object relations theory" (see Chapter 3 for a discussion of the origins of object relations theory in "Mourning and melancholia"). However, many of the components of Freud's theory of internal object relations contained in "Mourning and melancholia" are presented only in rudimentary form and often, in all probability, without Freud's awareness of the theoretical implications of his ideas. In considering the ques- tion of how one person's ideas concerning what is true influence those of others, we routinely adopt a diachronic (chronological, sequential) perspective in which the thinking of one person (for example, Freud), is seen as influencing the thinking of contemporaries and those who follow temporally (for example, Klein, Fairbairn, Guntrip, and Bion). Despite the seeming self-evidence of the merits of such an approach, I believe it may be of value to call into question this conception of authorship and influence. In reading "Mourning and melancholia," if one listens carefully, I believe one can hear the voice of Melanie Klein in Freud's discussion of the "internal world" of the melancholic. Freud posits that the structure of the unconscious internal world of the melancholic is determined by a defensive dual splitting of the ego leading to the creation of a stable unconscious internal object relationship between the "critical agency" (later to be termed the superego) and a part of the ego identified with the lost or abandoned object:

> The melancholic's disorder affords . . . [a view] of the constitution of the human ego. We see how in [the melancholic] one part of the ego sets itself over against the other, judges it critically, and, as it were, takes it as its object . . . What we are here becoming acquainted with is the agency commonly called "conscience" . . .
>
> (Freud, 1917b, p. 247)

In saying that the reader can hear Klein's voice (her concept of internal objects and internal object relations) in this and many other passages of "Mourning and melancholia," I am suggesting that influence does not occur exclusively in a chronologically "forward" direction. In other words, influence is not only exerted by an earlier contribution on a later one; later contributions affect our reading of earlier ones. One needs Klein to understand Freud, just as one needs

Freud to understand Klein. Every piece of analytic writing requires a reader who assists the author in conveying something of what is true, something that the author knew, but did not know that he knew. In so doing, the reader becomes a silent co-author of the text.

While this form of mutual influence of earlier and later contributions (mediated by the reader) is undoubtedly important, I would like to focus for a moment on another sort of influence that ideas exert on one another – often spanning great stretches of time, both chronologically forward and backward. Turning once again to the the example of the influence of Klein's ideas on Freud's, and vice versa, I am suggesting that the ideas Klein formulated in 1935 and 1940 on the subject of internal object relations may already have been available to Freud in 1915[1] and were utilized by him (unwittingly) in writing "Mourning and melancholia." Though he used the ideas, he could not think them. To say this is to entertain the possibility that the ideas that we think of as Klein's and as Freud's are creations of both and neither. The ideas that each articulated are formulations of the structure of human experience, a structure, a set of truths, which psychoanalysts and others attempt to describe, but certainly do not create.

Bion, I believe, held similar views on the question of the temporal bi-directionality of influence of ideas on one another:

> You can look at this [the inconsolable cries of a baby in his mother's arms immediately after his birth] as you like, say as memory traces, but these same memory traces can also be considered as a shadow which the future casts before [an anticipation of the future in the present as opposed to memories of the past] . . . The caesura [of birth] that would have us believe; the future that would have us believe; or the past that would have us believe – it depends on which direction you are travelling in, and what you see.
>
> (Bion, 1976, p. 237)

The future, for Bion, is as much a part of the present as is the past. The shadow of the future is cast forward from the present and is cast backward from the future onto the present – "it depends on which direction you are travelling in" (Bion, 1976, p. 237). (A great many questions regarding the relationship of an author to "his" or "her" ideas, and of the relationships among past, present and future ideas, will have to be left in a suspended state for the time being, pending a discussion of what we, as psychoanalysts, mean when we say something is true.)

II What's true?

The foregoing discussion of temporal bi-directionality of influence (Whose idea was it?) is inseparable from the question: "What's true?" I will take as a premise for my discussion of this question the idea that there is something true to human emotional experience which an analyst may accurately sense and communicate to a patient in words that the patient may be able to utilize. In assuming that there is something potentially true (or untrue) about psychoanalytic formulations and verbal interpretations of human emotional experience, it follows that emotional experience has a reality, a truth,[2] to it that is independent of the formulations or interpretations that the patient or the analyst may impose on it (Bion, 1970).

The idea that the truth is independent of the investigator lies at the core of the scientific method and is taken for granted in natural science. In molecular biology, for example, it seems self-evident that Watson and Crick did not create the double helical structure of DNA. That structure pre-existed their formulation of it: DNA has a double helical structure regardless of whether they or any other scientific investigator discern it (and provide evidence for the formulation).

The double helix is a structure that can be "seen" – albeit by inanimate objects (machines) that offer us the illusion that the human eye is capable of seeing the structure itself. In psychoanalysis, we do not have machines with which to see (even in illusory ways) psychological structures; we have access to psychological "structures" only insofar as they are experienced in the medium of unconscious, preconscious and conscious dreaming, thinking, feeling and behaving. We give shape to these structures in the metaphors that we create (e.g. the archaeological metaphor of Freud's topographic model or the metaphor constituting Freud's structural model which involves an imaginary committee comprised of the id, the ego and the superego attempting to deal with external and internal reality). And yet, there is something real (non-metaphorical) that psychoanalytic formulations – whether they be in the realm of metapsychology, clinical theory or interpretations offered to a patient – are measured against and that "something" is our sense (our "intuition," [Bion, 1992, p. 315]) of what is true to a given experience. In the end, it is emotional response – what feels true – that has the final word in psychoanalysis: thinking frames the questions to be answered in terms of feelings.

The analyst's feelings regarding what is true are mere speculations, however, until they are brought into relation to something external to the psychic reality of the analyst. The patient's response to an interpretation – and in turn, the analyst's response to the patient's response – serve a critical role in confirming or disconfirming the analyst's sense of what is true. This methodology represents an effort to ground psychoanalytic truth in a world outside the mind of the analyst. It takes at least two people to think (Bion, 1963). The "thinking" of one person on his or her own may be interminably solipsistic or even hallucinatory, and it would be impossible for a solitary thinker to determine whether or not this is the case.

Nevertheless, despite the analyst's efforts to ground what he feels to be true in a discourse with others, human beings are highly disposed to treat their beliefs as if they were truths. So who gets the last word on what is true? How are the various "schools" of psychoanalysis to be differentiated from cults, each of which is certain it knows what is true? I will not attempt to address directly these questions concerning how we develop some degree of confidence regarding the question of what is true. Instead, I will respond indirectly by offering some thoughts about what I think we, as analysts, mean when we say something is true (or has some truth to it). If we have an idea about what we mean when we say something is true, we may gain some sense of how we go about differentiating what is true from what is not.

As a starting point for thinking about what we mean when we say an idea is true, let us return to the idea that there are things that are true about the universe (including the emotional life of human beings) that pre-exist and are independent of the thinking of any individual thinker. In other words, thinkers do not create truth, they describe it. Thinkers from this perspective are not inventors, they are participant observers and scribes.

A comment made by Borges in an introduction to a collection of his poems comes to mind here:

> If in the following pages there is some successful verse or other, may the reader forgive me the audacity of having written it before him. We are all one; our inconsequential minds are much alike, and circumstances so influence us that it is something of an accident that you are the reader and I the writer – the unsure, ardent writer – of my verses [which occasionally capture something true to human experience].
>
> (Borges, 1923, p. 269)

Borges and Bion are in agreement; truth is invented by no one. For Bion (1970), only a lie requires a thinker to create it. What is true already exists (e.g., the double helical structure of DNA) and does not require a thinker to create it. In Bion's terms, psychoanalysis prior to Freud was "a thought without a thinker" (Bion, 1970, p. 104), that is, a set of thoughts that are true, "waiting" for a thinker to think them. Psychoanalytic conceptions of what is true to human emotional experience were not invented by Freud any more than the heliocentric solar system was invented by Copernicus.

Nonetheless, from a different vantage point, thinking thoughts that are expressive of what is true alters the very thing that is being thought. Heisenberg brought this to our attention in the realm of quantum physics. It is equally true in psychoanalysis and the arts that in interpreting or sculpting or making music, we are not simply unveiling what has been present all along in latent form; rather, in the very act of giving humanly sensible form to what is true to an emotional experience, we are altering that truth.

Shapes in nature do not have names; they do not even have shapes until we assign them visual categories of shapes that we are capable of imagining. Entities

65

in nature simply are what they are before we assign them a place in our system of symbols. So despite (or, in addition to) what was said earlier about the independence of the double helical structure of DNA from those who formu-lated it, Watson and Crick did alter the structure of DNA – they named its structure, and in that sense, gave it shape. The truth of the name of the shape was borne out by its power to give humanly sensible and humanly comprehensible organization to what had formerly lacked coherence. However, the fact of the creation of coherence is not a sufficient basis for establishing the truth of an idea. Religious systems create coherence. The truth of an idea, both in natural sciences and in psychoanalysis, rests on evidence brought to bear on an idea. Evidence consists of a set of observations (including the emotional responses of participant observers such as psychoanalysts working in the analytic setting) of the way things work (or fail to work) when one applies the idea/hypothesis to actual lived or observed experience.

In sum, we require what Bion (1962a) refers to as "binocular vision" (p. 86) – perception from multiple vantage points simultaneously – to articulate what we mean by the truth in psychoanalytic terms. What is true is a discovery as opposed to a creation; and yet in making that discovery, we alter what we find, and in that sense create something new. Nothing less than the psychoanalytic conception of the therapeutic action of the interpretation of the unconscious depends on such a view of the truth and the transformations effected in naming it. The analyst in making an interpretation (which has some truth to it and is utilizable by the patient) gives verbal "shape" to experience that had once been non-verbal and unconscious. In so doing, the analyst creates the potential for a new experience of what is true which is derived from the patient's inarticulate unconscious experience.

III Saying something one believes to be true

Let us pause a moment to take stock of what has been said thus far. Aside from issues of an author's narcissism, it is immaterial who it is that articulates something that is true – what is important is that a thought that is true has "found" a thinker who has made it available for a patient or a colleague to use. Neither does it matter, or even make sense to ask, "Whose idea was it?" What does matter in psychoanalysis – and it matters greatly – is finding words with which to say something that has a quality that is true to lived experience (whether it be an interpretation offered to a patient or a contribution made by an analyst to the analytic literature).

In this effort to say something that is true, the analyst must overcome Freud and the entire history of psychoanalytic ideas as well as the history of the analysis of the patient with whom he is working. In a somewhat whimsical aside made during a consultation, Bion spoke of the role of preconception in his clinical work: "I would [rely on theory only] . . . if I were tired and had no idea what was going on" (1978, p. 52). For Bion (1975), every session is the beginning of an analysis with a new patient. He was fond of saying that a patient may have had a wife and two children yesterday, but today he is single.

An analyst must also overcome himself in his written communications of ideas that he feels may have some truth to them. When analytic writing is good, the author is able to avoid getting in the reader's way by being too much of a personal presence in the writing. It makes for a very unrewarding experience for the analytic reader when the real topic of the paper one is reading is the author himself and not what the author is saying or what is being created by the reader in the act of reading.

Borges said of Shakespeare that he had a capacity equaled by no other writer to make himself transparent in his poems and plays. In his work, there is no one between the art and the audience. Borges wrote in a parable about Shakespeare (Borges' Shakespeare):

> There was no one in him; behind his face . . . and his words, which were copious, fantastic and stormy, there was only a bit of coldness, a dream dreamt by no one . . . History adds that before or after dying he [Shakespeare] found himself in the presence of God and told Him: "I who have been so many men in vain want to be one and myself." The voice of the Lord answered from a whirlwind: "Neither am I any one; I have dreamt the world as you dreamt your work, my Shakespeare, and among the forms in my dream are you, who like myself are many and no one.'
>
> (1949, pp. 248–249)

This rendering of Shakespeare as "a person with no one in him" is a harrowing picture of a human life; and yet I find that this portrayal of Shakespeare's relationship to his writing offers the psychoanalyst something to emulate in the sense of making himself available to becoming everyone in the patient's life (transferentially) and no one (a person who is content not to be noticed, not to be attended to). Borges' depiction of Shakespeare captures something of the task faced by an analyst in not inserting himself – his cleverness, his agility of mind, his capacity for empathy, his unerring choice of *le mot juste* – between the patient (or reader) and the interpretation.

In trying to stay out of the way of patients (or readers) in their efforts to discern something true, the analyst strives in his use of language and ideas to be both emotionally present and transparent. There was little that Borges more deplored in literature than "local color" (1941b, p. 42) and little that Bion more deplored in analytic interpretations than the analyst's explicit or implicit claim that the interpretation reflected the unique qualities of "*his* knowledge, *his* experience, *his* character" (Bion, 1970, p. 105) – his own "local color."

Literary critic, Michael Wood, speaking of the place of the writer in his or her writing, observes, "To write is not to be absent but to become absent; to be someone and then go away, leaving traces" (1994, p. 18). How better to describe what we, as psychoanalysts, strive for in making interpretations. We offer interpretations not for the purpose of changing the patient (which would be to attempt to create the patient in our own image), but to offer the patient something that has some truth to it, which the patient may find useful in doing conscious, preconscious and unconscious psychological work. Accompanying any psychological growth achieved in this way, we find not the signature of the analyst (i.e., his presence), nor his absence (which marks his presence in his absence), but traces of him as someone who was present and has become absent, leaving traces. The most important traces the analyst leaves are not the patient's identifications with him as a person, but traces of the experience of making psychological use of what the analyst has said and done and been.

IV What's true and for whom?

What is true to the relatively stable structure of human nature in general, and to an individual personality in particular, is neither bound by time nor place nor culture – even allowing for the influence of a wide range of value systems, forms of self-consciousness, religious beliefs and customs, forms of familial ties and roles, and so on. For example, there are no political or cultural borders separating human beings in the experience of the pain felt following the death of a child, the fear of bodily mutilation, the anguish of recognizing that one's parents and ancestors do not have the power to insulate themselves or their children from life's dangers and the inevitability of death. A culture may afford forms of defense against (or ways of evading) the pain of loss; or may provide traditions, myths and ceremonies that facilitate grieving; or may create rituals that help (or interfere with) efforts to loosen one's hold on infantile wishes. Whatever the cultural influences may be in a given instance, our responses to the basic human tasks of growing up, aging and dying, take place in cycles of love and loss; of dreaming oneself into existence and confronting the full force of the constraints of external reality; of feats of daring and the search for safety; of wishes to identify with those one admires and the need to safeguard (from one's own wishes to identify) the undisrupted evolution of one's self; and on and on.

These human tasks and the cycles in which they are played out contribute to a body of experience that I believe to be true of all humankind. It seems that paradoxically what is true is timeless, placeless and larger than any individual; and yet alive only for an instant and unique to the set of circumstances constituting that moment of lived experienced by one person. In other words, in an analysis, what is universally true is also exquisitely personal and unique to each patient and to each analyst. An analytic interpretation, in order to be utilizable by the patient, must speak in terms that could only apply to that patient at that moment while at the same time holding true to human nature in general.

I am reminded here of another comment by Borges:

> though there are hundreds and indeed thousands of metaphors to be found, they may all be traced back to a few simple patterns. But this need not trouble us, since each metaphor is different: every time the pattern is used, the variations are different.

(1967, p. 40)

Borges' observation is itself a metaphor suggesting that there are only a handful of qualities that make us human and that every person who has ever lived or who ever will live is an absolutely unique being made up of variations on a very small number of human qualities. And in that sense we are all one.

V What's true and whose idea is it in an analytic session?

What has been said thus far concerning what we, as analysts, mean when we say something is true remains pure abstraction until it is grounded in the lived experience of analytic work. As an analyst, I am not striving for Absolute Truth in what I say to a patient; I consider myself fortunate if once in a great while the patient and I arrive at something that is "very close/To the music of what happens" (Heaney, 1979, p. 173). The relative truths arrived at in poetry (and in psychoanalysis) represent "a clarification of life – not necessarily a great clarification, such as sects and cults are founded on, but a momentary stay against confusion" (Frost, 1939, p. 777). In the following account of a piece of analytic work, the patient and I strive to make psychological use of such momentary stays.

Mr V phoned me asking for a consultation concerning his wish to begin analysis with me. We set up a time to meet and I gave him detailed instructions about how to get to the waiting room of my office suite which is located at the ground level of my home. Just before the appointment time we had agreed upon, I heard a person (whom I assumed to be Mr V) opening the side door of my house. There is a short passageway between that door and a glass–paned interior door which is the entrance to the waiting room. I anticipated hearing the waiting room door open, but instead I heard the person walk back to the door to the outside, which was followed by a period of quiet lasting a minute or two. He – the footfalls sounded like those of a man – repeated this pattern of walking to the waiting room door and then returning to the door to the outside where he remained for another couple of minutes.

I found this man's movements distracting and intrusive, but also intriguing. Ms M, the patient who was with me in my consulting room, commented that someone, probably a new patient, seemed to be pacing in the hallway.

Immediately after Ms M left my office by a door that exited into the same passageway in which the man had been walking, I heard shuffling of feet and the voice of a man mumbling words of apology. I quickly went to see what was going on and for the first time encountered Mr V, a tall man of stocky build in his early forties. I said, "Mr V, I'm Dr Ogden," and motioning toward the glass-paned door, "Please have a seat in the waiting room." He had a sheepish, but slightly bemused expression on his face as I spoke.

Then, about five minutes later, when it came time for Mr V's session, I went to the waiting room and showed him to my consulting room. Once he was settled in his chair and I in mine, Mr V began by telling me that he had been thinking about beginning an analysis for some time, but "one thing and another" had caused him to delay. He then began to tell me about how he had been referred to me. I interrupted saying that there was a great deal that had already occurred in the session and that it would be important for us to talk about it before he and I could meaningfully talk about anything further. He looked at me with the same bemused expression I had observed in the passageway. I went on to say to Mr V that of all the ways he might have introduced himself to me, the one he had arrived at took the form of what had occurred in the passageway. So it seemed to me that it would be a shame not to take seriously what he had been trying to tell me about himself in that introduction.

There was a short pause after I finished speaking during which I had a fleeting memory (in the form of an emotionally intense series of still images) of an incident from my childhood. A friend, R, and I were playing on a frozen pond imagining ourselves to be Arctic explorers – we were both about eight years old at that time. The two of us ventured too close to an area which unbeknownst to us was not solidly frozen. R fell through the ice and I found myself looking down at him floundering in the freezing-cold water. I realized that if I were to get down on my hands and knees to try to pull him out, the ice would probably give way under me too and we both would be in the water unable to get out. I ran to a small island in the middle of the pond to get a long branch that I saw there. When I got back to R, he took hold of one end of the branch and I was able to pull him out of the water.

In the reverie, I pictured us (in a way that felt like peering intently into a photograph) standing there silently on the ice, R numb in his cold, wet clothes. As this was occurring, I felt a combination of fear and guilt and shame about his having fallen through the ice. The pond was much closer to my house than to his and I felt I should have known the signs of weak ice and should have protected him from falling through. The shame was in part connected with the fact that I had run away from him (the reality that I was running to get a branch with which to try to pull him out did not diminish the shame). But for the first time, it occurred to me on looking back on this event that there was shame felt by both of us about his being dripping wet as if he had wet his pants.

70

It had been years, perhaps a decade, since I had thought of that incident. While recalling these events in the session with Mr V, I felt sadness in response to the image of R and me becoming so separate and alone in the fear and shame that I assume he had felt, and that I know I had felt, after the accident. This had been no Tom Sawyer-Huck Finn adventure. R (I imagine) and I experienced our fear as well as our shame separately: we each felt stupid for having walked on the thinly frozen section of the pond and cowardly for having been so afraid. He and I never once mentioned the incident to one another afterwards nor did I ever tell anyone other than my mother about it.

These fleeting thoughts and feelings occupied only a moment of time, but were an emotional presence as I went on to say to Mr V that from the sound of his footsteps in the passageway, I suspected that he had been in some turmoil as he approached our first meeting. (Even as I was saying them, these words – particularly "turmoil" and "approached" – felt stiffly "therapeutic" and lifeless to me.)

Mr V responded by telling me that when we spoke on the phone, he had written down the directions I had given him about how to get into the waiting room from the outside of the house, but on arriving he found that he had forgotten to bring the scrap of paper on which he had written the instructions. When in the passageway between the door to the outside and the door to the waiting room, he was not sure whether the door with the glass panes was the waiting room door. He vaguely remembered my having mentioned a glass-paned door, but there was another door (the exit door from my consulting room), so not knowing what to do, he went back to the door to the outside. (The door to the outside has an opening in its upper third which is divided by vertical wooden spindles with wide spaces between them.) Mr V said that as he stood inside the passageway, peering out through the "bars" of the door, the daylight seemed blinding. He had felt as if he were in a prison in which, over a long span of time, his eyes had become so acclimated to the dark that he could not tolerate daylight. So he turned and went back to the glass-paned door and stood in front of it uncertain as so whether or not he should go in. He then returned to the outer door and stood for a while more looking from what felt like a great distance at the people outside who had lives they led in ways he could not imagine.

I told Mr V that I thought that he had not had a way, other than through his actions in the passageway, to convey to me what it felt like to him to be coming to meet with me. I said that without words he had told me how alone he felt in the no-man's land of the passageway. He felt barred both from coming in to see me to begin analysis and from going out and living as he imagined the people outside are able to do. The patient responded in a strikingly monotone voice, "Yes, I feel like a visitor everywhere, even with my family. I don't know how to do and say what seems to come naturally to other people. I'm able to keep that fact a secret at work because I am very good at what I do [there was a note of haughtiness in his voice here]. People are afraid of me at work. I think it's because I am abrupt. I don't know how to chat."

The patient in the first part of the hour tended to move to generalizations about experience outside of the session, while I periodically re-directed his attention to what had occurred and what was in the process of occurring in the session. About halfway through the hour, Mr V seemed to become interested in, and less fearful about, discussing what had occurred at the very beginning of the session. He said he had felt startled, first by the woman and then by me, as she and I came out of my office into the passageway. "I felt caught doing something I shouldn't have. No . . . that's not right. I felt caught at being weird and clueless about what everyone else knows."

After a brief pause, Mr V went on to say with little feeling in his voice, "I've learned to use my detachment from other people to my advantage in business because I can see things from an outside point of view. Being removed allows me to be ruthless because I say and do things to people that other people don't do in business. Either they don't think to do it or they don't want to . . . I'm not sure which. In a stand-off, I'm never the first to flinch." I said to the patient in a series of short comments that I thought that he was telling me that he was afraid that his extraordinary capacity for detachment and ruthlessness would make it impossible for him to be present in his own analysis; in addition, I said I thought he was suggesting that it was very likely that I would be frightened and repelled by him to the point that I would want nothing to do with him.

There was then another silence of several minutes duration which felt like a long time at such an early stage of the work. But it did not feel like an anxious silence, so I let it go on. During this silence, my mind "returned" to the reverie concerning the incident from my childhood. This time I experienced the childhood scene quite differently – I had a far greater sense of seeing and feeling things from inside of the two of us (R and me). This reverie experience was not that of a series of still images, but of a lived experience unfolding. I felt a good deal more of what it had been for me to be an eight-year-old boy on that frozen pond in winter. It was a state of mind that was a combination of living in a day dream made up of sensations that have such great immediacy that there is no room (or desire) to think. Things just happen, one after another. The events on the pond now had the emotional impact of a balloon exploding – not only had R fallen through the ice, we both were hit in the face with a blast of reality that annihilated the dreamy aspect of exploring on the frozen pond/Arctic Circle. It felt to me in the reverie that I had no choice but to become in an instant someone who could do the things that had to be done. R was in the water. I had to become someone I feared I could not be, someone more grown-up than I was. I did not feel the least bit heroic in the experience constituting this (second) reverie; I felt a bit disconnected from myself, but mostly I felt keenly aware that I was in over my head.

72

By this time Mr V had broken the silence and had begun to tell me about having been in therapy when he was in college. He had not been able to make friends and felt terribly homesick. The patient said that it had been a real stretch for his parents to pay for the therapy. After some time, I said to Mr V that I thought that when he realized in the passageway that he had forgotten the directions he had written down, he felt embarrassingly child-like and that for him to behave or even feel like a child is a very shameful thing. The patient said nothing in response to my comment, but the tension in his body visibly diminished. We sat quietly for a while. (It seemed to me that Mr V was worried that being in analysis would be a stretch for him – in a great many ways.) He then said, "Outside there, I felt so lost." There was softness to Mr V's voice as he spoke these words, a quality of voice that I had not heard from him, a softness that would prove to be a rarity in the course of the next several years of his analysis. (I was aware that the patient's feeling that there was an "outside there," was also a feeling that there was beginning to be an "inside here" – inside the analytic space, inside the relationship with me – in which he did not feel as lost.)

VI Discussion

Mr V's initial analytic meeting began in earnest about ten minutes before we actually met for the first time. His communications were made in the medium of sounds that echoed through the rest of the initial meeting and from there down the labyrinthine corridors of the analysis as a whole.

In my first interaction with Mr V in the passageway, I responded to his anxious non-verbal communications by identifying myself as Dr Ogden, thus naming not only who I was, but also what I was and why I was there. I firmly, but not coldly, directed him to the waiting room. The effect of my intervention was to both interrupt Mr V's communications in the medium of action (over which he appeared to have little, if any, control) and to define the geographic space in which analysis was to take place.

In his manner of speaking to me once he was in the consulting room, Mr V seemed to ignore – and seemed to invite me to ignore – the events that had transpired in the passageway. I soon interrupted Mr V's second introduction of himself. In telling him that I viewed his actions in the passageway as a way of telling me about his fears about beginning analysis, I was conveying to him the fact that I took him seriously in his unconscious efforts to be heard. My interpretation represented a continuation of my introducing myself to him as a psychoanalyst and my introducing him to psychoanalysis. Implicit in what I was doing and saying was the idea that the unconscious speaks with a quality of truthfulness that is different from, and almost always much richer than, what the conscious aspect of ourselves is able to perceive and convey. I was also introducing myself to the patient as a psychoanalyst for whom his behavior in the passageway did not represent an infraction of "analytic rules"; rather, it represented intense, urgent communications of some things he unconsciously believed to be true about himself which he felt were important for me to know from the very outset.

Mr V's reflexive response to what I said was to give me the sheepish, bemused smile I had noticed in the passageway. He seemed to be showing me in his facial expression a mixture of what felt like abject surrender and arrogant defiance, a particular mix that I would learn over time was characteristic of the patient as a response to certain types of narcissistic anxiety. A brief silence followed in which I recalled in a series of still images, my boyhood experience with R when he fell through the ice. Particularly vivid in this reverie were feelings of fear, shame, isolation and guilt. A component of the shame in this reverie experience seemed new and very real to me: the idea/feeling that R's pants were wet because, in his fear, he had soaked them with urine.[3] Just as immediate, for me, as my image of R (with whom I thoroughly identified) in his shamefully soggy clothes, were my feelings of sadness concerning the isolation from one another that R and I had felt.

The emotional field of the session was changed in ways that I was only beginning to understand by my having lived the experience of this reverie in the context of what was occurring at an unconscious level between the patient and me. Following my reverie, Mr V gave a detailed, but affectively muted account of his experience in the passageway. He recounted having forgotten the scrap of paper on which he had written the directions I had given him; he went on to describe his inability either to enter the waiting room or to leave the passageway (which felt like a prison) and enter the blindingly lit world outside. My response to Mr V's depiction of himself in the passageway involved an effort to re-state what he had said in slightly different language and with expanded meaning. My intention was to underscore the ways in which the patient knew, but did not know that he knew, about another level of the experience he had just described. My use of the phrase "no-man's land," in re-telling the story Mr V had told me, suggested that he not only felt alone, but also unmanly and like no one. Moreover, in my making explicit that entering the waiting room was, for him, emotionally equivalent to beginning analysis, I was also suggesting that entering the waiting room posed the danger of entering into the potentially crazed world of the unconscious. (The patient's fear of the out-of-control world of the unconscious was already alive in me in the form of the frightening reverie image of R falling through the ice.)

An important shift occurred mid-way through the session, when Mr V, on his own, returned to the experience in the passageway. He made a delicate, yet critical emotional distinction in saying, "I felt caught doing something I shouldn't have" and then corrected himself: "No that's not right . . . I felt caught at being weird and clueless about what everyone else knows." There was a sense of relief in Mr V's voice in being able to say something that felt true (and significant) to his emotional experience. The patient then quickly retreated to the familiar ground of reliance on defensive omnipotence in asserting that he could be more ruthless in business than others dare to be (or even aspire to be) and that he was never the first to flinch.

The long silence that occurred at that juncture was a period in which it felt to me that the patient and I were able to do a good deal of unconscious psychological work that had not been possible up to that point in the session. My reverie during that silence was one in which the memory of the incident on the pond was re-worked in the context of what had transpired in the session in the interval between the first and second reverie. In contrast with the first reverie which I experienced as a series of still photographic images, the new reverie was an experience of an unfolding event that felt much closer to and more alive with the feelings of an eight-year-old boy. In that sense, it was a far more understanding, more compassionate rendering of the event. I was less fearful of experiencing the feelings that the reverie involved.

At the heart of the second reverie was a feeling of myself as a boy being called upon (and calling upon myself) to do something that I was afraid was emotionally and physically beyond me. This feeling of shameful immaturity was a new version of a feeling I had experienced in the earlier reverie in identifying with R as an eight-year-old boy who was behaving like a baby (who, in fantasy, had peed in his pants).

The more emotionally accepting affective state generated in the second reverie allowed me to listen differently to Mr V. I heard his reference to his parents' financial "stretch" (in paying for his therapy while he was homesick at college) as a comment on how he was feeling at that moment in the analysis. I told him that I thought he had felt painfully and embarrassingly like a child when he was in the passageway and that for him to behave like or even feel like a child was a very shameful thing. He did not respond with words, but there was visible relaxation in his body. Not only my words, but also the feeling-tone of my voice reflected my own experience in the reveries in which I had felt painfully over my head and shamefully infantile.

Mr V then said, "Out there, I felt so lost." These words were alive in a way that was different from anything that the patient had previously said or done, not only because of the softness of his voice as he spoke these words, but also because of the words themselves. How different it would have been if he had said, "In the passageway, I felt lost" or "Out there, I felt very lost," instead of "Out there, I felt so lost." There is something unmistakable about the truth when one hears it.

In closing this clinical discussion, I would like to address briefly the question of who it was who came up with the ideas that felt true in the analytic session I have described. As I have previously discussed (Ogden, 1994a, 1997b, 2001a), I view the analyst's reverie experience as a creation of an unconscious intersubjectivity that I call "the analytic third," a third subject of analysis, which is jointly, but asymmetrically, created by analyst and patient.[4] It would make no sense to me to view the reveries involving my boyhood experience on the pond solely as reflections of the work of my unconscious or solely a reflection of the unconscious work of the patient.

From this perspective it is impossible (and meaningless) to say that it was my idea or the patient's that was conveyed in the interpretation of Mr V's feeling shamefully infantile and over his head when "caught" being clueless both about how to enter analysis and how to be present and alive in the world. Neither Mr V nor I alone was the author of this and the other understandings (relative emotional truths) that were spoken and unspoken during this initial session. If there was an author, it was the unconscious third subject of analysis who is everyone and no one – a subject who was both Mr V and I, and neither of us.

6

Reading Bion

Bion's writing is difficult. And yet, one consistently finds that to rely on "translations" of Bion into more accessible prose is to diminish, if not completely ablate, the impact of Bion's radical reconfiguration of many of the fundamental tenets of psychoanalytic theory and technique. In this chapter, I will offer some thoughts on how one might approach reading Bion in a way that renders his ideas utilizable, and yet, at the same time, attends closely to the language in which his ideas are cast.[1]

Key to my reading of Bion is the idea that a common source of confusion in reading his work derives from a failure to recognize that there are two contrasting periods of Bion's opus which are based on overlapping, yet distinctly different sets of assumptions regarding psychoanalysis. The writing from the two periods requires different ways of reading which generate different experiences in reading. I refer to the two periods as "early" and "late" Bion. The former consists of all of Bion's writing up to and including *Learning from Experience* (1962a); the latter begins with *Elements of Psycho-Analysis* (1963).[2] It is tempting to view the late work as an evolution from the early work. My own reading of the two periods of Bion's work, however, leads me to a different conclusion. To my mind, the late work, while incorporating and assuming a thorough familiarity with the early work, represents a radical departure from it. As will be discussed, the experience of reading early Bion generates a sense of psychoanalysis as a never-completed process of clarifying obscurities and obscuring clarifications, which endeavor moves in the direction of a convergence of disparate meanings. In contrast, the experience of reading Bion's later work conveys a sense of psychoanalysis as a process involving a movement toward infinite expansion of meaning.

In this chapter, I take as starting points the experience of reading two passages, one from *Learning from Experience* (1962a) and the other from *Attention and Interpretation* (1970). In these passages, Bion suggests to the reader the way he would like his "early" and "late" writing to be read. In this endeavor, I am not attempting to arrive at what Bion "really meant"; rather, I am interested in seeing what use – clinically and theoretically – I am able to make of my own experiences of reading early and late Bion. On the basis of many comments made by Bion in the last decade of his life, there can be little doubt that this is the way Bion would hope to have all of his work read: "The way that *I* do analysis is of no importance to anybody excepting myself, but it may give you some idea of how *you* do analysis, and that *is* important" (1978, p. 206).

In the final section of this chapter, I present a detailed account of an analytic session and then discuss the analytic experience from a point of view that is informed by Bion's work, particularly his late work.

I Bion on reading early Bion

In the introduction to *Learning from Experience*, Bion carefully and patiently explains to the reader how he would like his book to be read:

> The book is designed to be read straight through once without checking at parts that might be obscure at first. Some obscurities are due to the impossibility of writing without pre-supposing familiarity with some aspect of a problem that is only worked on later. If the reader will read straight through, those points will become clearer as he proceeds. Unfortunately obscurities also exist because of my inability to make them clearer. The reader may find the effort to clarify these for himself is rewarding and not simply work that has been forced on him because I have not done it myself.
>
> (1962a, p. ii)

In this passage, Bion, in a highly compact way, provides several thoughts on reading his text. First, the reader must be able to tolerate not knowing, getting lost, being confused and pressing ahead anyway. The words "obscure," "obscurities" (mentioned twice), "clearer" and "clarify" (each also used twice), pile up in these five sentences. What it is to learn from experience (or the inability to do so) will be something for the reader to experience first-hand in the act of reading this book – an experience in reading that does not simply "progress" from obscurity to clarification, but resides in a continuous process of clarification negating obscurity and obscurity negating clarification. Bion, not without an edge of irony and wit, suggests that "the reader may find [it] . . . rewarding" to attempt to "clarify [obscurities]" for himself "not simply . . . because I have not done it myself." In other words, if the reader is to engage in something more than "merely reading" (1962a, p. ii) this book, he must become the author of his own book (his own set of thoughts) more or less based on Bion's. Only then will the reader have generated the possibility of learning from his experience of reading.

Bion (1992), in a note to himself, a "cogitation" which in all probability was written during the period in which he was writing *Learning from Experience*, elaborates on the idea that the act of reading is an experience in its own right to be lived and learned from: "The book will have failed for the reader if it does not become an object of study, and the reading of it an emotional experience itself" (1992, p. 261). In another "cogitation," Bion presents his "early" conception of how analytic writing works, and by implication, how he would like to be read. (The passage I will cite immediately follows a brief page-and-a-half account of an analytic session that includes detailed observations of both Bion's emotional experience and that of his psychotic patient.)

I do not feel able to communicate to the reader an account that would be likely to satisfy me as correct. I am more confident that I could make the reader understand what I had to put up with if I could extract from him a promise that he would faithfully read every word I wrote; I would then set about writing several hundred thousand words virtually indistinguishable from what I have already written in my account of the two sessions. In short, I cannot have as much confidence in my ability to tell the reader what happened as I have in my ability to do something to the reader that I have had done to me. I have had an emotional experience; I feel confident in my ability to recreate [in writing] that emotional experience, but not to represent it.

(1992, p. 219)

In this elegant prose – Bion is a difficult writer, not a bad writer – Bion envisions psychoanalytic writing as an effort not to report, but to create an emotional experience that is very close to the emotional experience that the analyst has had in the analysis. In this passage, and the clinical account that precedes it, Bion is doing what he is saying; he is demonstrating as opposed to describing. In the clinical work presented, the psychotic patient, who in reality "may commit a murder" (p. 218), whispers at the end of the session, "I will not stand it" (p. 219). Bion comments that "there seems to be no reason why such sessions should ever come to an end" (p. 219). (In this last sentence, Bion is speaking from the patient's point of view and in so doing communicates what is unstated in the sentence and in the session, and yet is ominously present in both: In a psychotic field, time is obliterated and endings are arbitrary and unexpected – and consequently may incite actual murder.)

In his comments following the clinical account, Bion succeeds at getting into the language itself, something of his experience of being with the patient. He imagines writing several hundred thousand words about "what I had to put up with" and "extract[ing]" – a word that is alive with the sound of violent coercion – "a promise" from the reader. The promise "that [the reader] would faithfully read every word I wrote" is "extract[ed]" before the reader knows of the forthcoming onslaught of words – words that add nothing to what Bion has already said. The experience in reading that Bion is imagining is a tortured one that would never come to an end and may incite murderous feelings in the reader. In this way, Bion creates something like the emotional experience he lived with his patient, as opposed to "represent[ing]" it, (i.e., describing it). To describe the analytic experience would be to mispresent it because the emotional vantage point of the writing would be from a place outside of the experience, when, in fact, Bion's experience was simultaneously generated from within and outside of the analytic event: "We [analysts] have to be able to have these strong feelings *and* be able to go on thinking clearly even when we have them" (Bion, 1978, p. 187).

To summarize, in offering his thoughts on how he would like *Learning from Experience* to be read, Bion portrays a state of mind (generated in the act of reading) that is at once open to living an emotional experience and at the same time actively engaged in clarifying obscurities and obscuring (i.e. releasing itself from the closures of) clarifications. These mental activities in concert constitute a substantial part of what it means to learn from experience, both in reading and in the analytic situation. This is at core a hermeneutic approach in which there is a progressive dialectical movement between obscurity and clarification which moves toward, though never achieves, closure.

II A mixing of tongues

In examining the emotional experience of reading *Learning from Experience*, it is impossible to ignore the strangeness of the language and terminology that Bion employs. In part, he is attempting to cleanse analytic terminology of the ossified and ossifying "penumbra of associations" (1962a, p. 2) that have accrued over time, and instead, to use "meaningless term[s]" (p. 3) (such as alpha- and beta-elements) unsaturated by previous usage. However, not all of the strangeness of Bion's language is attributable to that effort to generate analytic language disencumbered by accretions of meaning. A large part of the opacity of Bion's writing derives from his mixing the language, notational systems and conceptions belonging to the fields of mathematics and symbolic logic (for example, the concepts of functions and factors) with the language of psychoanalysis.

Bion refers again and again to the set of ideas that he is developing in *Learning from Experience* as "a theory of functions" (p. 2) and devotes much of the first two chapters of the book to explaining what he means by a function. Bion uses the term "function" to refer to a form of mental operation that determines the outcome of every psychic event governed by that mental operation. In mathematics, addition, subtraction, multiplication and division (along with differential and integral calculus) are functions. So when we say $a + b = c$, we are saying that when the function of addition (represented by the + sign) is in operation, we know the relationship among a, b and c. In *Learning from Experience*, Bion is attempting to release psychoanalytic thinking from the confines of the specifics of a given analytic event, thus facilitating the delineation of a small number of essential psychological functions which are very roughly analogous to mathematical functions. This conception of the task of analytic theory accounts for the highly abstract nature of Bion's writing and the paucity of clinical material presented in his work. (Mathematics, according to Bion, could not have developed as a system of logical thought if it required the presence of 5 oranges to add 2 and 3 to make 5.)

The way the mind works, from the perspective of "early Bion," centrally involves alpha-function – the function of transforming raw sensory data (termed "beta-elements") into units of meaningful experience (termed "alpha-elements") which can be linked in the process of thinking and stored as memory. As discussed in Chapter 4, for Bion, dreaming is a form of alpha-function. Dreaming is not a reflection of the differentiation of the conscious and unconscious mind, but the psychological activity/function which generates that differentiation (and consequently is responsible for the maintenance of sanity itself). If one is unable to transform raw sensory data into unconscious elements of experience (alpha-elements), one is unable to dream, unable to differentiate being awake and dreaming; consequently, one is unable to go to sleep and unable to wake up; "hence the peculiar condition seen clinically when the psychotic patient behaves as if he were in precisely this state" (Bion, 1962a, p. 7). (See Chapter 4 for a detailed clinical illustration of analytic work related to the state of not being able to dream.)

I have elected to discuss briefly Bion's theory of functions not only because it represents a critically important aspect of Bion's thinking, but, as important, because it serves as an illustration of the sort of work involved in reading early Bion. The reader must move with Bion as he borrows the concept of function from mathematics and symbolic logic and in so doing moves analytic theory-making to a very high level of abstraction. (This aspect of reading Bion strongly carries over to the experience of reading his theory of transformations and his conception of the grid in his late work.) At the same time, he replaces familiar psychoanalytic models and terminology (e.g., Freud's topographic and structural models and Klein's model of the paranoid schizoid and depressive positions) with intentionally meaningless terms such as alpha-function, beta-elements and alpha-elements. Moreover, as if this were not sufficiently dislocating for the reader, Bion alters the meanings of everyday words that the reader thought he understood (for instance, the idea of dreaming, going to sleep and waking up).

What is involved in the experience of reading early Bion includes an oscillation between clarification of obscurities and the obscuring of clarifications in a progressive hermeneutic cycle. In addition, the experience of learning from the reading of that work has something of an *Alice in Wonderland* quality. The whole world of psychoanalytic theory feels different as one reads Bion because it is different. Words and ideas once familiar are made foreign, and the foreign made "familiar" (of the family of psychoanalytic ideas). How fundamentally different current analytic theory and practice is as a consequence of Bion's early work: for instance, the notion of the patient's attacks on his own meaning-generating function (i.e., the capacity for thinking, feeling, dreaming and so on); the conception of the patient's attacks on the analyst's capacity for reverie; and the delineation of forms of countertransference acting out in which the analyst fearfully and defensively attacks his own and/or the patient's capacity to think.

III Bion on reading late Bion

In approaching Bion's late work I will again make use of some of his comments on how he would like his work to be read as a port of entry into his thinking – this time, focusing on *Attention and Interpretation* (1970). A problem posed by Bion's later work is immediately apparent in the "advice" that he offers the reader early in that book. Just as the experience of reading served as a medium in which *learning from experience* was brought to life in Bion's early work, so too in *Attention and Interpretation*, the living experience *in reading*[3] is used to convey what cannot be said in words and sentences:

> the reader must disregard what I say until the O of the experience of reading has evolved to a point where the actual events of reading issue in his [the reader's] interpretation of the experiences. Too great a regard for what I have written obstructs the process I represent by the terms "he becomes the O that is common to himself and myself".
>
> (1970, p. 28)

The reader is thrown directly into the fire of not knowing and is advised not to evade this state by holding "too great a regard for what I have written." And at the same time, the question is inescapable: What is meant by "the O" of an experience? Bion uses such terms as "the thing in itself," "the Truth," "Reality," and "the experience" to convey a sense of what he has in mind by O. But since Bion also insists that O is unknowable, unnamable, beyond human apprehension, these nouns are misleading and contrary to the nature of O. In introducing O to the analytic lexicon, Bion is not proposing another reality "behind" the apprehensible one; he is referring to the reality of what is, a reality that we do not create, a reality that precedes and follows us, and is independent of any human act of knowing, perceiving or apprehending.

The language Bion uses in offering thoughts about reading his late work suggests that the reader is best armed with capacities for the negative. What cannot be known can be addressed only in terms of what it is not: "The reader must disregard what I say" and not hold "too great a regard for what I have written." The "instructions" to the reader in *Learning from Experience* were founded in part on the notion that the reader must let go of what he thought he knew in order to enter a progressive cycle of knowing and not knowing. In contrast, Bion's instructions in *Attention and Interpretation* focus on "disregard[ing]" what Bion is *saying* altogether, for such adherence to statements *about* experience obstructs the reader's access to the actual events (the O of the experience) of reading.

The reader is told that if he is able to remain *in* the experience of reading, his state of mind will "issue in his [the reader's] interpretation of the experiences" (1970, p. 28). There is a critically important ambiguity here to the word "experiences": is Bion referring to the analytic experiences he (Bion) has had with his patients that are now the subject of his text or are "the experiences" the reader's experiences in reading the text? Of course, it is both: Bion's experiences in analysis are conveyed not by writing *about* those experiences, but by using language in such a way that his experiences *in* analysis become the reader's experiences *in* reading. To the extent that the writing works, the irreducible, unverbalizable essence, the O, of each of the two experiences – the reader's experience in reading Bion and Bion's experiences in reading his patients – become at one with ("common to") one another. The reader "becomes the O that is common to himself [his experiences in reading] and myself [Bion's experiences *in* the analyses that he has conducted]" (p. 28). I am aware that in the previous sentences, I have been using the term O without having defined it. To my mind, this is the only way one can fruitfully approach the concept of O – by allowing its meanings to emerge (its effects to be experienced) as one goes. The effects are ephemeral and survive only as long as the present moment, for no experience can be stored and called up again. *We register experience (O) and are altered by it; we hold experience (O) in our being, not in our memory.*

Bion's choice of the word "interpretation" in his advice to the reader – "the actual events of reading issue in his interpretation of the experiences" – is an unexpected word given that the passage strongly privileges "being *in*" as opposed to "speaking *about*." But there is no getting around Bion's use of the nettlesome word "interpretation," which inescapably focuses on the analyst's formulation of what is true to the emotional experience occurring between patient and analyst. What Bion is struggling to convey, I believe, is that *psychoanalysis is most fundamentally an enterprise involving* "the emergence" *(p. 28) into the realm of knowing (K)*[4] *of the unsymbolizable, unknowable, inexpressible experience itself.* Bion's use of the word "emergence" lies at the core of an understanding of the relationship between the experience – the unknowable and unsymbolizable (O) – and the symbolizable, the apprehensible dimensions of experience (K).

An emergence is "an unforeseen experience" (*Oxford English Dictionary*). In terms of the relationship between O and K, experiences in K (i.e. experiences of thinking, feeling, perceiving, apprehending, understanding, remembering and bodily sensing) are "evolutions of O" (Bion, 1970, p. 27). Such evolutions of O are "unforeseeable" in the same way that consciousness is a wholly unforeseeable emergence from the electrical and chemical workings of the brain. There is absolutely nothing in the study of the physiology of the brain that would lead one to anticipate the experience of human consciousness. Similarly, there is nothing in the structure and physiology of the eye and its myriad connections with the brain that would allow us to anticipate the experience of vision.

The idea of "emergence" as a philosophical concept involves a conception of an interplay of forces at one level of complexity (e.g. neuronal clusters) that results in the generation of genuinely novel qualities (e.g., consciousness or vision) that are impossible to anticipate through the study of the individual units of either of the two levels of complexity (Tresan, 1996; Cambray, 2002). Though there is no evidence that Bion was familiar with this strand of philosophical thought (developed by a group of British philosophers in the first half of the twentieth century [McLaughlin, 1992]), to my mind, the philosophical concept of emergence closely corresponds to Bion's (1970) notion of the "emergence" of ("evolution" of) O in the realm of apprehensible, "sensible" experience (K).

In contrast to the apprehensible evolutions/emergences of O in K, the experience itself (O) simply is. The only verb suited to follow the sign O is some form of the verb to be; an experience in O is an experience of being and becoming. The interpretation as an act of becoming draws on and allows itself to be shaped by what is. One recognizes the truth when one hears it in music, sees it in sculpture, senses it in an analytic interpretation or a dream. One cannot say what it is, but in sculpture, for example, the sculptor creates aesthetic gestures that direct the viewer toward O; in psychoanalysis, the analyst and analysand make "things" (analytic objects such as interpretations) in verbal and non-verbal form which emerge from, and gesture toward, what is true to the present emotional experience.

The O (the truth of what is) is highly specific to the emotional situation generated by a particular analyst and a particular patient at a given moment of analysis. And, at the same time, the truth of what is (the O of that experience) involves a truth that holds for all humankind from the "past unknown to us . . . [to the] whole present . . . which envelops us all; . . . [to the] future as yet uncreated" (Borges, 1984, p. 63).[5] The O of these universal truths is emergent in and constitutive of our very being and traverses all time, for truth and time are related only by coincidence. In this sense, O is that set of inarticulate, universal human truths that we live, but do not know; it is what we hear in music and poetry, but cannot name; it is who we are in dreaming, but cannot communicate in the telling of the dream.

O is a state of being-in-the-present-moment, a moment that "Is too much for the senses, / Too crowding, too confusing – / Too present to imagine" (Frost,

1942a, p. 305). Our capacity for being-in-the-present is "obstructed" by the humanly understandable wish to protect ourselves from its blinding glare. We seek shelter from the O of the present moment in the shadows of memories of what we think we know because it has already been and in our projections of the past into the future.

It is not surprising, given what has been said, that the interpretations that "issue from" the experiences of reading late Bion (or from experiences with a patient in analysis) will inevitably be disappointing and will involve a sense of loss. Bion (1975) has observed that interpretations are regularly followed by a feeling of depression (I would say sadness). What has been lost in the interpretation is the ineffable, inexpressible experience of what is true to the emotional experience. Literary critic, Lionel Trilling (1947), in response to the question, "What does *Hamlet* mean?" stated that *Hamlet* does not mean "anything less than *Hamlet*" (p. 49). *Hamlet* is *Hamlet*; O is O; "The world, unfortunately, is real; I, unfortunately, am Borges" (Borges, 1946, p. 234).

In sum, Bion's late work requires a type of reading quite different from what is demanded by his early work. Reading the earlier work involves experiencing a cycle in which obscurities are progressively clarified; those clarifications are then reopened to new confusions that demand further clarifications of a sort that lend coherence (at a greater depth) to the experience of reading, and so on. The overall "shape" of dialectical movement is that of movement toward a never attained convergence of sets of meanings. And at the same time, reading early Bion includes a hefty dose of the experience of strange brilliance and brilliant strangeness – for example, his concept of beta-elements, alpha-function, the idea of being unable to fall asleep or wake up, and the application of mathematical concepts to psychoanalysis.

Bion's later work provides a markedly different experience in reading. If reading early Bion is an experience of movement toward convergence of disparate meanings, the experience of reading late Bion is an experience of movement toward an infinite expansion of meaning. The experience of reading late Bion is one in which the reader is pushed to his limits and then some in his effort to sustain a state of active receptivity to every possible experience in reading. If reading early Bion is an experience of learning from experience, reading late Bion is an experience of disencumbering oneself of the deliberate use of all that one has learned from experience in order to be receptive to all that one does not know: "There is nothing more to be said about what you [the analyst] are prepared for; what you know, you know – we needn't bother with that. We have to deal with all that we don't know" (Bion, 1978, p. 148).

I will conclude this section of the chapter with two brief observations. First, it might be said that the reading of early Bion and late Bion are experiences that stand in dialectical tension with one another. But, on the basis of what I have discussed thus far, I believe that it is more accurate to describe the two

Reading Bion

experiences in reading as fundamentally different in nature. The two stand as different "vertices" (Bion, 1970, p. 93) from which to view the analytic experience. They give stereoscopic depth to one another as opposed to conversing with one another.

Second, in reading late Bion, it is important to bear in mind that O is not a philosophical, metaphysical, mathematical or theological conception; it is a psychoanalytic concept. Bion is exclusively interested in the psychoanalytic experience: he is concerned only with the analyst's task of overcoming what he knows in order to be at one with what is, the O of the analytic experience at any given moment. His conception of the analytic state of mind (reverie) is one in which the analyst makes himself as open as possible to experiencing what is true and attempts to find words to convey something of that truth to the patient. Transcendence of self on the part of the analyst is by no means an end in itself and is of no use whatever to the patient; the analyst's task is that of saying something "relatively truthful" (Bion, 1982, p. 8) regarding the emotional experience occurring at any given moment of the analysis which the patient might be able to use consciously and unconsciously for purposes of psychological growth.

IV A preface to an analytic experience

Before offering a clinical example illustrating the use in analytic practice of some of the ideas discussed above, it is necessary to introduce one additional concept (taken from Bion's late work) which, for me, represents a critical bridge between Bion's conception of the way the mind works and the experiential level of the psychoanalytic process. What I am referring to is a distinction that Bion makes in *Attention and Interpretation* between two types of remembering:

> We are familiar with the experience of *remembering* a dream; this must be contrasted with dreams that float into the mind unbidden and unsought and float away again as mysteriously. The emotional tone of this experience is not peculiar to the dream: thoughts also come unbidden, sharply, distinctly, with what appears to be unforgettable clarity, and then disappear leaving no trace by which they can be recaptured. I wish to reserve the term "memory" for experience related to conscious attempts at recall. These [conscious attempts at recall] are expressions of a fear that some element, "uncertainties, mysteries, doubts", will obtrude.
>
> (1970, p. 70)

For Bion, "memory" is an anxiety-driven use of the mind that interferes with the analyst's capacity to be receptive to what is true to the emotional experience, the O of that experience, as lived in the present moment. By contrast,

86

Dream-like memory is the memory [memories that float into the mind unbidden] of psychic reality and is the stuff of analysis . . . the dream and the psycho-analyst's working material both share dream-like quality.

(pp. 70–71)

Thus, when the analyst is doing genuine analytic work, he is not "remembering," that is, not consciously attempting to know/understand/formulate the present by directing his attention to the past. Rather, he is experiencing the analysis in a "dream-like" way – he is dreaming the analytic session. An analyst consulting with Bion (1978) commented that she found his observations to be of such great value that she worried that she would not be able to remember them all. Bion replied that he hoped she would not remember anything of what he had said, but that it would make him happy if one day while in an analytic session, something of what had occurred in the consultation came back to her in a way that felt like an unexpected recollection of a dream and perhaps that dream-like remembering might be of help to her in saying something to the patient that the patient could make use of.

V On not being "an analyst"

Mr B, during a phone call in which we set up our first meeting, told me that he did not want analysis. In the initial session, he repeated his wish not to be in analysis and added that he had seen "the school shrink" while in college for a few sessions for insomnia, but could not remember the man's name. I chose not to ask for clarification of what Mr B meant by "analysis" and why he was so set against it. My decision to desist from intervening in this way was based on a sense that to have done so would have been to ignore what this patient was trying very hard to tell me: he did not want me to be "an analyst" without a name, an analyst who conducted himself in a manner that represented the outcome of his experience with other patients. In my work with him, I was not to be who I thought I was or who I previously had been to any other person or to myself.

At the end of the first session, I suggested possible times to meet again later in the week. Mr B opened his appointment book and told me which of the times would be best for him. I continued this method of arranging one future meeting at a time over the next several months; it seemed to suit Mr B in that period of our work. In the course of the first several months, a schedule of daily meetings became established. In the second or third session, I told Mr B that I thought I would be able to work best with him if he used the couch; we began working in that manner in the subsequent session. Mr B told me that using the couch was a little strange, but it suited him too.

The patient at first said almost nothing about the present circumstances of his life, including how old he was. He mentioned his wife, but it was not clear how long they had been married, what sort of marriage it was or whether they had any children. I did not feel any inclination to inquire; his way of being with me and my way of being with him at that juncture seemed to be a more important form of communication than could be achieved through my making inquiries. When, on occasion, I did ask a question, the patient responded politely and earnestly, but the questions and responses seemed only to distract Mr B and me from the task of introducing ourselves to one another at an unconscious level.

The "patient" – an odd word because Mr B was not a patient in a way that was familiar to me – never told me why he had come to see me. I do not think he himself knew. Instead, he told me "stories" of events in his life that were important to him, but which did not "make a point" in the sense of illustrating a dilemma or describing a form of psychological pain concerning which he needed or wanted my help. I found his stories interesting: Mr B regularly surprised me in that in his accounts he portrayed himself as a person who is just a little removed and a little "off" in an utterly unselfconscious (and endearing) way. For example, he told me that when he was in fourth grade, there was a new girl, L, in his class who had recently moved to the town in which he grew up. Her father had died the previous year, a fact that Mr B found "riveting, mysterious and incomprehensible." He and L became very attached to one another; their relationship continued through the end of high school and into their first year of college. It was "very intense and very stormy."

An incident from this long relationship with L stood out in the patient's mind. The day after they had gone to a high school dance together, Mr B went to L's house to pick her up for a drive that they had arranged. When the patient rang the doorbell, L's mother came to the door and told him that L was not home. Mr B stood there for a moment frozen with disbelief. He told me that he then got into his car and drove for hours screaming in pain at the top of his lungs. Mr B went on to say that L, years later, had told him that she had felt so embarrassed about having been hung over from drinking with some girlfriends after he had dropped her off that she had asked her mother to tell him that she was not at home.

In my interventions during the first year or so of the analysis, I used words very close to those used by the patient, but with the emphasis shifted just a bit. For instance, in response to the account of L's mother's having told Mr B that L was not at home, I said, "How could you have known what was happening if you weren't being told the truth?" In speaking in this way, I was putting into words an idea and a set of feelings that addressed a good deal of what was happening in that phase of the analysis: I was underscoring the enormous importance to Mr B of saying what is true. I took the story of L's mother's lie as an unconscious expression of the patient's feeling that I could hurt him deeply by not being truthful with him, by playing the role of analyst as opposed to being myself as *his* analyst. My comment to Mr B was in part informed by a story he had told me months earlier: During a conversation that took place in a tenement, an albino cockroach scurried across Mr B's notepad. The patient said in a matter-of-fact way that he has not been bothered by the cockroach: "Where else would a cockroach live if not in a tenement? I was the visitor, not him."

As Mr B spoke of L's mother's lie, I wondered what I would do if one of my sons during his high school years, had asked me to lie to one of his close friends. I could not imagine doing so, except under extraordinary circumstances. My mind wandered to a set of experiences with G, my best friend when we were ten or eleven years old. His family had moved to the United States from Australia only a couple of years earlier. I recalled G's habit of greatly exaggerating a story in his telling of it. When confronted with irrefutable evidence of his exaggeration, he would say, "I were only kidding." I was aware even as a child that G was using the word "were" instead of the word "was," and with that one exception, he said things the same way the rest of us did (albeit with an Australian accent). I found his habit of distorting the truth to be embarrassing in its desperateness. This was a particularly painful memory for me during the session with Mr B. because it was so closely linked with memories of my own acts of dishonesty in childhood which were still a source of shame for me. There had been a number of occasions when I had shown off to G's mother by mentioning a book I had read or a piece of national news I had heard about. I had not felt the need to posture in this way with the parents of any other of my friends. I remembered, too, how surprised I was that G called his mother by her first name. I emerged from this reverie with a deep sense of sadness for G, who had lived under such enormous pressure (both internal and external) to be someone he was not for his mother. Who he was – and who I was – was simply not good enough.

As my attention returned to Mr B, he was telling me about riding his bicycle to school when he was about ten years old. He would stop periodically along the way and put a leaf or a stone or a bottle cap in a particular place – for example, between the boards of an old fence or in a cave that was "no more than a dug out hole under a big rock." On the way home from school, he would retrieve these objects. Mr B recalled with pleasure the feel of the wind on his face as he rode home on his bicycle and the feeling of amazement he felt that during the whole time that he was in school these things were there "spending the day doing something else" and were waiting for him on his way home. It seemed that the important thing about this childhood experience was the sense of security that Mr B derived from knowing that these things were alive (alive with meaning) just as he was alive in his own being at school. The carefully placed objects had an existence that went on in his absence: the stone and the leaf and the bottle cap went on being what they were. As Mr B was telling me the story, the sound and cadences of his words reminded me of lines from a

Borges (1957) prose poem: "All things long to persist in their being; the stone eternally wants to be a stone and the tiger a tiger" (p. 246).

In listening to Mr B's story about the stones and leaves and bottle caps remaining themselves while he was at school (in conjunction with my reverie regarding G and his mother), it occurred to me that Mr B had been frightened as a child – and now with me – that his connection with his mother (and me) felt thin, not based on truths that remain true, truths that can be taken utterly for granted, love that remains love, a mother who persists in her being as a mother *all the time*. I said to Mr L, "It seems to me that you felt – although I don't know if you would put it this way – that L's mother was not motherly either to L or to you in lying to you. There is something about being a mother that doesn't go together with lying. It's not a matter of ethics or sentimentality; it's a feeling that a mother, when she's being a mother, is telling the truth, she *is* the truth." Mr B and I were silent for a few minutes until the end of the session.

Some months later, as Mr B was beginning to be able to speak more directly about feelings, he told me that as a child, there were long stretches of time during which he felt frightened that he would come home and find that his mother had been taken over by aliens – she would no longer be his mother even though she looked exactly like his mother. He would try to devise questions, the answers to which only his real mother would know. He said, "I remember vividly that fear that I felt as a kid and only now recognize the loneliness that went with it. But at this moment, all I feel is cold – not distant or remote – but physically cold, as if the temperature in the room has suddenly dropped by 25 degrees."

VI Discussion

The work with Mr B began with an unconscious request that I not be a generic analyst, and instead be a person capable of not knowing who I am and who he is. Only in that way would I be able to be open to what I do not know, i.e., to the O of who he is (and of who I am with him). If I was to be of any help to Mr B, I would have to invent a psychoanalysis that bore his name, his being. This would stand in contrast to the therapy provided by his previous therapist who has no name, i.e. who did not make a therapy with Mr B that had their names on it.

Mr B's unconscious request was a reasonable one that every patient makes, but for him, it held particular significance that derived from his own life experience including his relationship with his mother. Her state of being-his-mother felt not only unreliable, but untrue to him. In the early part of the analysis, this quality of his experience of his mother was brought to life in a great many forms. Through his unique way of being with me, Mr B unconsciously communicated to me the importance to him of people being genuinely (truth-fully) present with one another. He refused to adapt himself to what he imagined to be the prescribed form in which he was to take the role of a patient consulting a doctor concerning a malady for which he was seeking treatment. Rather, Mr B seemed just to be there and I was to respond only to who he was. It was his being (the O of who he is) that I was to experience, not a pre-packaged substitute for O in the form of my preconceptions (or his) about analysis. My efforts to do so, for instance by setting up only one meeting at a time, did not feel like contrivances, but rather, as the way it had to be and should be with Mr B at that point. I listened (with genuine interest) to his stories without trying to ferret out what the story was "really about"; the story was not about anything; the story was the story; O is O.

I attempted to speak to Mr B in a way that emerged from what was true to the emotional experience that was occurring. In speaking of the lie that L's mother told the patient, I spoke of the confusion, the inability to think, in the face of a lie: "How could you have known what was happening if you weren't being told the truth?" Every interpretation that an analyst makes is directed to his own experience as well as that of the patient. In this instance, my interpretation served as a starting point for a reverie involving G's desperate exaggerations and my own feelings of shame concerning my own childhood emotional dishonesty (posturings). My feelings of shame were followed by sadness regarding G's (and my own) sense of inadequacy in the eyes of his mother. His ungrammatical use of the word "were" in his saying "I were only kidding," now, in retrospect, seems to have been a complex event reflecting the breakdown of language and thinking in the face of his own efforts to become a lie, i.e. to be someone other than who he was. Perhaps also the word "were" in his statement represented a strangulated beginning of a plea to his mother, a wish that she were a different kind of mother, a mother who could sincerely love him as he was, not as she wished he were.

Reverie, like dreaming, while often involving great complexity of feeling, is nonetheless a form of unmediated or barely mediated experience. In reveries and dreams there is almost nothing of a reflective self. Even when an apparently observing self is a figure in a dream, that figure has no greater powers of observation than any other figure in the dream (including the narrator). In this sense, I view reverie as an *experience of what is* at an unconscious level in the analytic relationship – the O of the unconscious of the analyst and analysand living in the experience of the unconscious analytic third (Ogden, 1994a, 1994c, 1999a). The reverie concerning my friend, G, and his mother was not *about* the unconscious events occurring in the analysis at that point – it *was* the O of the unconscious experience at that point.

Mr B's response to my interpretation concerning his inability to know what was happening in the face of a lie took the form of his telling me a story about his way of reassuring himself as a child that things (and, by extension, people) remain true to who they are when out of sight. (As time went on, the patient's stories became more layered with meaning. This was reflected, for example, in the way the story of the hidden stones and leaves lent itself more naturally to verbally symbolic interpretation.)

I spoke to Mr B in terms of the feelings and images that he had introduced (and in terms of feelings that I had experienced in my reverie). I told him that I thought he felt that L's mother had not been a mother to L or to him in lying to him and that being a mother is somehow to be what is true. Of course I was also saying indirectly that being an analyst is also somehow to be what is true, i.e. that it is my job to attempt to become and say the truth, the O of the emotional experience at a given juncture of the analysis. (The knowledge that the analyst cannot possibly succeed in this effort to say and be what is true was addressed by Bion in response to the self-criticism of an analyst who was presenting a session to him. The analyst was chastising herself for the inadequacy of her interpretations. Bion, nearly eighty at the time, commented: "If you had been practising analysis as long as I have, you wouldn't bother about an inadequate interpretation – I have never given any other kind. That is real life – not psycho-analytic fiction" [1975, p. 43]).

It seems fitting to conclude this chapter with a mention of Mr B's comments about his childhood fear that he would find that his mother was no longer really his mother. His experience at this juncture captures the difference between *remembering an experience* (his recollecting his childhood fear and his new aware-ness of the loneliness that was part of it), and *becoming the O of that experience* (his feeling chilled, his becoming that chilling experience).

On holding and containing, being and dreaming

Winnicott's concept of holding and Bion's idea of the container–contained are for each of these analysts among his most important contributions to psychoanalytic thought. In this light, it is ironic that the two sets of ideas are so frequently misunderstood and confused with one another. In this chapter, I delineate what I believe to be the critical aspects of each of these concepts and illustrate the way in which I use these ideas in my clinical work.

I view Winnicott's holding as an ontological concept that is primarily concerned with being and its relationship to time. Initially the mother safeguards the infant's continuity of being, in part by insulating him from the "not-me" aspect of time. Maturation entails the infant's gradually internalizing the mother's holding of the continuity of his being over time and emotional flux.

By contrast, Bion's container–contained is centrally concerned with the processing (dreaming) of thoughts derived from lived emotional experience. The idea of the container–contained addresses the dynamic interaction of predominantly unconscious thoughts (the contained) and the capacity for dreaming and thinking those thoughts (the container).

Throughout the discussion, it must be borne in mind that the concepts of holding and the container–contained stand not in opposition to one another, but as two vantage points from which to view an emotional experience.

I Holding

As is the case for almost all of Winnicott's seminal contributions, the idea of holding is a deceptively simple one (Ogden, 2001c). The word "holding," as used by Winnicott, is strongly evocative of images of a mother tenderly and firmly cradling her infant in her arms, and when he is in distress, tightly holding him against her chest. Those psychological/physical states of mother and infant are the essential experiential referents for Winnicott's metaphor/concept of holding.

The importance of the impact of maternal holding on the emotional growth of the infant would be disputed by very few psychoanalysts. However, the significance to psychoanalytic theory of Winnicott's concept of holding is far more subtle than this broad statement would suggest. Holding, for Winnicott, is an ontological concept that he uses to explore the specific qualities of the experience of being alive at different developmental stages as well as the changing intrapsychic-interpersonal means by which the sense of continuity of being is sustained over time.

Being in the infant's time

The earliest quality of aliveness generated in the context of a holding experience is aptly termed by Winnicott (1956) "going on being" (p. 303), a phrase that is all verb, devoid of a subject. The phrase manages to convey the feeling of the movement of the experience of being alive at a time before the infant has become a subject. The mother's emotional state entailed in her act of holding the infant in his earliest state of going on being is termed by Winnicott "primary maternal preoccupation" (1956). As is true of the infant's state of going on being, primary maternal preoccupation is a subjectless state. It must be so because the felt presence of the mother-as-subject would tear the delicate fabric of the infant's going on being. In primary maternal preoccupation, there is no such thing as a mother. The mother "feel[s] herself into her infant's place" (Winnicott, 1956, p. 304) and in so doing ablates herself not only as the infant experiences her, but also, to a large degree, as she experiences herself. Such a psychological state is "almost an illness" (p. 302) – "a woman must be healthy in order both to develop this state and to recover from it as the infant releases her" (p. 302).

A principal function of the mother's early psychological and physical holding includes her insulating the infant in his state of going on being from the relentless, unalterable otherness of time. When I speak of the otherness of time, I am referring to the infant's experience of "man-made time": the time of clocks and calendars, of the four-hour feeding schedule, of day and night, of the mother's and the father's work schedules, of weekends, of the timing of maturational landmarks spelled out in books on infant development, and so on. Time in all of these forms is a human invention (even the idea of day and night) that has nothing to do with the infant's experience; time is other to him at a stage when awareness of the "not-me" is unbearable and disruptive to his continuity of being.

In her earliest holding of the infant, the mother, at great emotional and physical cost to herself, absorbs the impact of time (e.g. by foregoing the time she needs for sleep, the time she needs for the emotional replenishment that is found in being with someone other than her baby, and the time she needs for making something of her own that is separate from the infant). In effect, the mother's earliest holding involves her entering into the infant's sense of time, thereby transforming for the infant the impact of the otherness of time and creating in its place the illusion of a world in which time is measured almost entirely in terms of the infant's physical and psychological rhythms. Those rhythms include the rhythms of his need for sleep and for wakefulness, of his need for engagement with others and his need for isolation, the rhythms of hunger and satiation, the rhythms of breathing and heartbeat.

The mother's early holding of the infant represents an abrogation of herself in her unconscious effort to get out of the infant's way. Her unobtrusive presence "provides a setting for the infant's constitution to begin to make itself evident, for the developmental tendencies to start to unfold, and for the infant to experience spontaneous movement and become the owner of the sensations that are appropriate to this early phase of life" (Winnicott, 1956, p. 303). The mother's risking psychosis in providing selfless "live, human holding" (Winnicott, 1955, p. 147) allows the infant to take his own risk in beginning to come together as a self. That earliest moment of coming together "is a raw moment; the new individual feels infinitely exposed" (1955, p. 148).

Clinical example

In the following clinical account, the form of holding just described plays a central role.

Ms R startled when I met her in the waiting room for our first session. She said hello without making eye contact, and in a stiff awkward way, walked from the waiting room into my consulting room. She lay down on the couch without our ever having discussed her using the couch. Ms R turned her head toward the wall (away from me and the little bit of light coming through the closed window blinds). The patient blurted out in clumps of words the fact that she had begun to have panic attacks for which she could find no cause. She told me that she was not able to work or to be a mother to her two adolescent children. Almost in passing, she told me that her mother had died six months earlier – "She was old and sick and it was for the best."

When I made a comment or asked a question in the early stages of this analysis, the patient startled in the way she had in the waiting room when we first met. I did not comment on this behavior and learned quickly to say almost nothing during the sessions. Even the sound of my moving in my chair was experienced by the patient almost as if I had slapped her.

It was necessary for me to remain as still and quiet as possible if Ms R was to be able to tolerate being with me. The patient, sensing my stillness (except for the sound and movement of my breathing), relaxed noticeably in the course of the first several sessions and ceased speaking altogether during our meetings for weeks afterwards. I did not experience the need to remain as quiet as I could as the outcome of the patient's tyrannical rule; rather, being with her reminded me of sitting in my younger son's bedroom when he was three years old as he fitfully lay in bed trying to fall asleep after having been awoken by a nightmare.

Quite the opposite of feeling put upon by Ms R (or by my son), I felt that my presence was like a soothing balm on a burn. While with the patient during a prolonged period of silence, I recalled that when my son began to be able to relax into sleep, his rhythm of breathing and my own became one. In my half-sleeping state during one of the nights I sat with him, I dreamt dreams in which my wife and children had disappeared. The dreams felt so real that it took me a bit of time on waking to recognize them as dreams.

In retrospect, I believe that during those nights with my son I was unconsciously becoming at one with him, physically and psychologically, breathing his rhythm of breathing, dreaming his fears. The hours spent by his bed remain with me as disturbing, tender experiences. In the session with Ms R, as I recalled that period of sitting with my younger son, a line from a poem by Seamus Heaney (1984) came to mind: "Never closer the whole rest of our lives" (p. 285). I felt that the patient needed of me what my very young son had needed. I was willing to be used in that way by Ms R when she was able to take the risk of drawing on me at such a depth.

In the reverie that included the thoughts about my son and the line from the Heaney poem, I was preconsciously talking to myself about the experience of selfless holding that Ms R needed. It was as much a physical experience (for me and, I believe, for her) as it was a psychological one.

The gathering of bits

As the infant grows, the function of holding changes from that of safeguarding the fabric of the infant's going on being to the holding/sustaining over time of the infant's more object-related ways of being alive. One of these later forms of holding involves the provision of a "place" (a psychological state) in which the infant (or patient) may gather himself together. Winnicott speaks of

> the very common experience of the patient who proceeds to give every detail of the week-end and feels contented at the end if everything has been said, though the analyst feels that no analytic work has been done. Sometimes we must interpret this as the patient's need to be known in all his bits and pieces by one person, the analyst. To be known means to feel integrated at least in the person of the analyst. This is the ordinary stuff of infant life, and an infant who has had no one person to gather his bits together starts with a handicap in his own self-integrating task, and perhaps he cannot succeed, or at any rate cannot maintain integration with confidence.
>
> (1945, p. 150)

Here, the earlier, physical/emotional type of holding has given way to metaphorical holding, the provision of a psychological space that depends upon the analyst's being able to tolerate the feeling "that no analytical work has been done." Winnicott demonstrates in the way he uses language what he has in mind. In saying, "Sometimes we must interpret this as the patient's need to be known in all his bits and pieces by one person, the analyst," Winnicott is using the word "interpret" to mean *not to give verbal interpretations to the patient*, and instead, simply, uninterruptedly to be that human place in which the patient is becoming whole.

This type of holding is most importantly an unobtrusive state of "coming together in one place" that has both a psychological and a physical dimension. There is a quiet quality of self and of otherness in this state of being in one place that is not a part of the infant's earlier experience of "going on being" (while held by the mother in her state of primary maternal preoccupation).

Internalization of the holding environment

The experience of transitional phenomena (Winnicott, 1951) as well as the capacity to be alone (Winnicott, 1958) might be thought of as facets of the process of the internalization of the maternal function of holding an emotional situation in time. In transitional phenomena, the situation that is being held involves the creation of *"illusory experience"* (Winnicott, 1951, p. 231, italics in original) in which there is a suspension of the question " *'Did you conceive of this or was it presented to you from without?' The important point is that no decision on this point is expected. The question is not to be formulated*" (Winnicott, 1951, pp. 239–240).

Winnicott views this third area of experiencing – the area between fantasy and reality – not simply as the root of symbolism, but as "the root of symbolism in time" (1951, p. 234). Time is coming to bear the mark of the external world that lies outside of the child's control, while at the same time being an extension of the child's own bodily and psychological rhythms. When the child's psychological state (whether as a consequence of constitutional make-up and/or trauma) is such that he cannot tolerate the fear evoked by the absence of his mother, the delicate balance of the sense of simultaneously creating and discovering one's objects collapses and is replaced by omnipotent fantasy. The latter not only impedes the development of symbolization and the capacity to recognize and make use of external objects, it involves a refusal to accept the externality of time. Consequently, the experience of being alive is no longer continuous; rather, it occurs in disconnected bursts: magic is a series of instantaneous phenomena.

The capacity to be alone, like the development of transitional phenomena, involves an internalization of the environmental mother holding a situation in time. The most fundamental experience that underlies the establishment of the capacity to be alone is "*that of being alone, as an infant and small child in the presence of [environmental] mother*" (Winnicott, 1958, p. 30, italics in original). Here, it is the function of the mother as holding environment (as opposed to the mother as holding object) that is in the process of being taken over by the infant or child. This development should not be confused with the achievement of object constancy or object permanence, both of which involve the formation of stable mental representations of the mother as object. Winnicott, in describing the development of the capacity to be alone, is addressing something more subtle: the taking over of the function of the maternal holding environment in the form of a child's creating the matrix of his mind, an internal holding environment.

Depressive position holding

The nature of Winnicott's concept of holding that has been implicit in the forms of holding that I have discussed thus far might be thought of as emotional precursors of the depressive position as Winnicott conceives of it. For Winnicott (1954a), the depressive position involves one's holding for oneself an emotional situation over time. Once the infant has achieved "unit status" (p. 269), he is an individual with an inside and an outside. The feeding situation at this point involves the infant's or young child's fear that in the act of feeding, he is depleting his mother (concretely that he is making a hole in the mother or the breast). (The child has in fact been depleting the mother all along as a consequence of the physical and emotional strain involved in her being pregnant with, giving birth to, and caring for him as an infant.) "All the while [during the feed and the digestive process that follows] the mother is holding the situation in time" (p. 269).

During the period of digesting the experience of the feed, the infant or small child is doing the psychological work of recognizing the toll that his (literal and metaphorical) feed is taking on his (now increasingly separate) mother. "This [psychic] working-through [of his feeling of having damaged his mother] takes time and the infant can only await the outcome [in a psychological state in which he is], passively surrendered to what is going on inside" (p. 269).

Eventually, if the infant or child has been able to do this psychological work, and if the mother has been able to hold the situation over time, the infant produces a metaphorical (and sometimes also an actual) bowel movement. An infant or a child whose gift is recognized and received by his mother "is now in a position to do something about that [fantasized] hole, the hole in the breast or body [of the mother] . . . The gift gesture may reach to the hole, if the mother plays her part [by holding the situation in time, recognizing the gift as a reparative gesture, and accepting it as such]" (p. 270).

Depressive position holding involves the mother's recognition of the infant's "unit status" (his coming into being as a separate person), her being able to tolerate her separateness from him, and psychically to hold (to live with) the truth of her infant's and her own changing status in relation to one another. She is no longer his entire world, and there is great pain (and also relief) for her in that loss. The emotional situation is creatively destructive in that the infant risks destroying the mother (by making a hole in her) in the act of taking from her what he needs to be able eventually to feed himself (i.e., to become a person separate from her).

In depressive position holding, the child is becoming a subject in his own right in the context of a sense of time that is more fully other to himself. The child recognizes that he cannot move people faster than they will move of their own accord nor can he shrink the time during which he must wait for what he needs or wants. Depressive position holding sustains the individual's experience of a form of being that is continuously transforming itself – an experience of remaining oneself over time and emotional flux in the act of becoming oneself in a form previously unknown, but somehow vaguely sensed.

II The container–contained

As is true of Winnicott's *holding*, Bion's (1962a, 1962b, 1970) *container–contained* is intimately linked with what is most important to his contribution to psychoanalysis. The idea of the container–contained addresses not what we think, but the way we think, i.e. how we process lived experience and what occurs psychically when we are unable to do psychological work with that experience.

The psychoanalytic function of the personality

Fundamental to Bion's thinking, and a foundation stone for his concept of the container–contained, is an idea rarely addressed in discussions of his work: "the psycho-analytic function of the personality" (1962a, p. 89). In introducing this term, Bion is suggesting that the human personality is constitutionally equipped with the potential for a set of mental operations that serves the function of doing conscious and unconscious psychological work on emotional experience (a process that issues in psychic growth). Moreover, by calling these mental operations "psycho-analytic," Bion is indicating that this psychological work is achieved by means of that form of thinking that is definitive of psycho-analysis, i.e. the viewing of experience simultaneously from the vantage points of the conscious and unconscious mind. The quintessential manifestation of the psychoanalytic function of the personality is the experience of dreaming. Dreaming involves a form of psychological work in which there takes place a generative conversation between preconscious aspects of the mind and disturbing thoughts, feelings and fantasies that are precluded from, yet pressing toward conscious awareness (the dynamic unconscious). This is so of every human being who has achieved the differentiation of the conscious and unconscious mind regardless of the epoch in which he is living or the circumstances of his life.

From one perspective, Bion's proposal of a psychoanalytic function of the personality is startling. Could he really mean that the personality system of human beings as self-conscious subjects is somehow designed to perform the functions described by a late nineteenth/early twentieth-century model of the mind? The answer, surprisingly, is yes: for Bion (1970), psychoanalysis before Freud was a thought without a thinker, a thought awaiting a thinker to conceive it as a thought. What we call psychoanalysis is an idea that happened to be thought by Freud, but had been true of the human psyche for millennia prior to Freud's "discovery" (Bion, 1970; Ogden, 2003b).[1]

Dream-thoughts and dreaming

In order to locate Bion's concept of the container–contained in relation to the larger body of his thinking, it is necessary to understand his conception of the role of dreaming in psychological life (see Chapter 4, for a clinical and theoretical discussion of Bion's conception of dreaming). For Bion, dreaming occurs both during sleep and waking life: "*Freud* [1933] says Aristotle states that a dream is the way the mind works in sleep: *I* say it is the way it works when awake" (Bion, 1959c, p. 43). Dream-thought is an unconscious thought generated in response to lived emotional experience and constitutes the impetus for the work of dreaming, i.e. the impetus for doing unconscious psychological work with unconscious thought derived from lived emotional experience.

Bion's (1962a) conception of the work of dreaming is the opposite of Freud's (1900) "dream-work." The latter refers to that set of mental operations that serves to disguise unconscious dream-thoughts by such means as condensation and displacement. Thus, in derivative/disguised form, unconscious dream-thoughts are made available to consciousness and to secondary process thinking. By contrast, Bion's work of dreaming is that set of mental operations that allows conscious lived experience to be altered in such a way that it becomes available to the unconscious for psychological work (dreaming). In short, Freud's dream-work allows derivatives of the unconscious to become conscious, while Bion's work of dreaming allows conscious lived experience to become unconscious (i.e. available to the unconscious for the psychological work of generating dream-thoughts and for the dreaming of those thoughts).

Thus, basic to Bion's thinking is the idea that dreaming is the primary form in which we do unconscious psychological work with our lived experience. This perspective, as will be seen, is integral to the concept of the container–contained. I will begin the discussion of that idea by tentatively defining the container and the contained.

The "container" is not a thing, but a process. It is the capacity for the unconscious psychological work of dreaming, operating in concert with the capacity for preconscious dream-like thinking (reverie), and the capacity for more fully conscious secondary process thinking. Though all three of these types of thinking – unconscious dreaming, preconscious reverie and conscious reflection – are involved in the containing function of the mind, Bion views the unconscious work of dreaming as the work that is of primary importance in effecting psychological change and growth. Bion (1978) urges the analyst not to be "prejudiced in favour of a state of mind in which we are when awake [as compared to the state of mind in which we are when asleep]" (p. 134). In other words, for Bion, the state of being awake is vastly overrated.

The "contained," like the container, is not a static thing, but a living process that in health is continuously expanding and changing. The term refers to thoughts (in the broadest sense of the word) and feelings that are in the process of being derived from one's lived emotional experience. While conscious and preconscious thoughts and feelings constitute aspects of the contained, Bion's notion of the contained places primary emphasis on unconscious thoughts.

The most elemental of thoughts constituting the contained are the raw "sense-impressions related to an emotional experience" (Bion, 1962a, p. 17) which Bion (1962a) calls "beta-elements" (p. 8). I have found no better words to describe these nascent thoughts than those used in a poem by Edgar Alan Poe (1848): beta-elements might be thought of as "Unthought-like thoughts that are the souls of thought" (p. 80).[2] These most basic of thoughts – thoughts unlinkable with one another – constitute the sole connection between the mind and one's lived emotional experience in the world of external reality. These unthought-like thoughts (beta-elements) are transformed by "alpha-function" (an as yet unknown set of mental operations) into elements of experience ("alpha-elements") that may be linked in the process of dreaming, thinking and remembering. (The "souls" of alpha-elements are the sense-impressions derived from lived emotional experiences.)

The lineage of the concept of the container–contained

Having begun the discussion of the container–contained by defining the container and the contained, I will briefly trace the development of Bion's ideas concerning the interplay of thoughts and thinking, of dream-thoughts and dreaming.

In his earliest psychoanalytic work, *Experiences in Groups* (1959b), Bion introduced the idea that thoughts (shared unconscious "basic assumptions") hold the power to destroy the capacity of a group for thinking. Bion elaborated the idea that thoughts may destroy the capacity for thinking in his essays that are collected in *Second Thoughts* (1967), most notably in "Attacks on linking" (1959a) and "A theory of thinking" (1962b). There, Bion introduced the idea that in the beginning (of life and of analysis) it takes two people to think. (In stark contrast to Winnicott – who is always the pediatrician – for Bion, his ideas/speculations concerning the psychological events occurring in the mother–infant relationship are merely metaphors – "signs" [Bion, 1962a, p. 96] – that he finds useful in constructing a "model" [p. 96] for what occurs at an unconscious level in the analytic relationship.)

The metaphoric mother–infant relationship that Bion (1962a, 1962b) proposes is founded upon his own revision of Klein's concept of projective identification: The infant projects into the mother (who, in health, is in a state of reverie) the emotional experience that he is unable to process on his own, given the rudimentary nature of his capacity for alpha-function. The mother does the unconscious psychological work of dreaming the infant's unbearable experience and makes it available to him in a form that he is able to utilize in dreaming his own experience.

A mother who is unable to be emotionally available to the infant (a mother incapable of reverie) returns to the infant his intolerable thoughts in a form that is stripped of whatever meaning they had previously held. The infant's projected fears under such circumstances are returned to him as "nameless dread" (1962a, p. 96). The infant's or child's experience of his mother's inability to contain his projected feeling state is internalized as a form of thinking (more accurately, a reversal of thinking) characterized by attacks on the very process by which meaning is attributed to experience (alpha-function) and the linking of dream-thoughts in the process of dreaming and thinking (Bion, 1959a, 1962a, 1962b).

Relocating the center of psychoanalytic theory and practice

When the relationship of container (the capacity for dreaming, both while asleep and awake) and contained (unconscious thoughts derived from lived emotional experience) is of "mutual benefit and without harm to either" (Bion, 1962a, p. 91), growth occurs in both container and contained. With regard to the container, growth involves an enhancement of the capacity for dreaming one's experience, i.e. the capacity for doing (predominantly) unconscious psychological work. The expansion of the containing capacity in the analytic setting may take the form of a patient's beginning to remember dreams to which he and the analyst have associations – associations that feel real and expressive of what is happening unconsciously in the analytic relationship. For another patient, expansion of the capacity for dreaming may be reflected in a diminution of psychosomatic symptomatology or perverse behavior in conjunction with an increase in the patient's capacity to experience feelings and be curious about them. For still another patient, enhancement of the containing function may manifest itself in the cessation of repetitive post-traumatic nightmares (which achieve no psychological work [Ogden, 2004b]).

The growth of the contained is reflected in the expansion of the range and depth of thoughts and feelings that one is able to derive from one's emotional experience. This growth involves an increase in the "penetrability" (Bion, 1962a, p. 93) of one's thoughts, i.e. a tolerance "for being in uncertainties, mysteries, doubts, without any irritable reaching after fact and reason" (Keats, 1817, quoted by Bion, 1970, p. 125). In other words, the contained grows as it becomes better able to encompass the full complexity of the emotional situation from which it derives. One form of the experience of the growth of the contained involves the patient's finding that a past experience takes on emotional significance that it had not previously held. For example, in the third year of analysis, an analysand felt for the first time that it was odd, and painful, to "recall" that his parents had not once visited him during his three-month hospitalization following a psychotic break while he was in college. (It could reasonably be argued that the new significance of the remembered event represents the growth, not of the contained, but of the container – the capacity for dreaming the experience. I believe both ways of thinking about the clinical example are valid: in every instance of psychological growth there is growth of both the container and the contained. Moreover, in attempting to differentiate between the container and the contained in clinical practice, I regularly find that the two stand in a reversible figure-ground relationship to one another.)

Under pathological circumstances, the container may become destructive to the contained resulting in a constriction of the range and depth of the thoughts one may think. For instance, the container may drain life from the contained, thus leaving empty husks of what might have become dream-thoughts. For example, pathological containing occurs in analytic work with a patient who renders meaningless the analyst's interventions (the contained) by reflexively responding with comments such as: "What good does that do me?" or "Tell me something I don't already know" or "What psychology book did you get that from?"

Another form of pathological containing occurred in the analysis of a schizophrenic patient that I have previously described (Ogden, 1980). During an early period of that analysis, the patient imitated everything I said and did, not only repeating my words as I spoke them, but replicating my tone of voice, facial expressions and bodily movements. The effect on me was powerful: the imitation served to strip away feelings of realness and "I-ness" from virtually every aspect of my mind and body. The patient was subjecting me to a tyrannizing form of containing that caused me to feel that I was losing my mind and body. Later in the analysis, when a healthier form of containing had been achieved, this pathological containing was understood as a replication (imitation) of the patient's unconscious sense of his mother's having taken over his mind and body, leaving him nothing of his own that felt real and alive.

Still another type of pathological containing takes the form of a type of "dreaming," which like a cancer, seems to fill the dream space and the analytic space with images and narratives that are unutilizable for psychological work. Potential dream-thoughts promiscuously proliferate until they reach the point of drowning the dreamer (and the analyst) in a sea of meaningless images and narratives. "Dreams" generated in this way include "dreams" that feel like a disconnected stream of images; lengthy "dreams" that fill the entire session in a way that powerfully undermines the potential for reverie and reflective thinking; and a flow of "dreams" dreamt in the course of months or years that elicit no meaningful associations on the part of patient or analyst.

Conversely, the contained may overwhelm and destroy the container. For example, a nightmare may be thought of as a dream in which the dream-thought (the contained) is so disturbing that the capacity for dreaming (the container) breaks down and the dreamer awakens in fear (Ogden, 2004b). Similarly, play disruptions represent instances when unconscious thoughts overwhelm the capacity for playing.

Bion's concept of the container–contained expands the focus of attention in the psychoanalytic setting beyond the exploration of conflict between sets of thoughts and feelings (e.g., love and hate of the Oedipal rival; the wish to be at one with one's mother and the fear of the loss of one's identity that that would entail; the wish and need to become a separate subject and the fear of the loneliness and isolation that that would involve, and so on). In Bion's hands, the central concern of psychoanalysis is the dynamic interaction between, on the one hand, thoughts and feelings derived from lived emotional experience (the contained), and on the other, the capacity for dreaming and thinking those thoughts (the container).

The aim of psychoanalysis from this perspective is not primarily that of facilitating the resolution of unconscious conflict, but facilitating the growth of the container–contained. In other words, the analyst's task is to create conditions in the analytic setting that will allow for the mutual growth of the container (the capacity for dreaming) and the contained (thoughts/feelings derived from lived experience). As the analysand develops the capacity to generate a fuller range and depth of thoughts and feelings in response to his experience (past and present) and to dream those thoughts (to do unconscious psychological work with them), he no longer needs the analyst's help in dreaming his experience. The end of an analysis is not measured principally by the extent of resolution of unconscious conflict (which has been brought to life in the transference–countertransference), but by the degree to which the patient is able to dream his lived emotional experience on his own.

In sum, container and contained, in health, are fully dependent on one another: the capacity for dreaming (the container) requires dream-thoughts; and dream-thoughts (the contained) require the capacity for dreaming. Without dream-thoughts one has no lived experience to dream; and without the capacity for dreaming, one can do no psychological work with one's emotional experience (and consequently, one is unable to be alive to that experience).

Clinical illustration

The following clinical example will serve to illustrate how I use the concept of the container–contained in analytic practice.

Ms N regularly began her daily sessions by telling me in great detail about an incident from the previous day in which she had made use of something I had said in recent sessions. She would then pause, waiting for me to tell her that she had made very good use of the insights she had gained from our analytic work. As the patient waited for me to say my lines, I would feel a form of anger that increased over the course of the years we worked together.

Even my anger felt not to be of my own making since the patient was well aware of the maddening effect that her controlling scripting had on me. ("Scripting" and "feeding me my lines" were metaphors that Ms N and I had developed to refer to her efforts to expunge her awareness of the separateness of our minds and of our lives. The metaphors also referred to the patient's feeling that her mother had treated her as an extension of herself. Perhaps in an effort to separate from her mother psychically, the patient developed anorexia nervosa in adolescence; the disorder continued to play an important role in her life from that point onward.)

Ms N used shopping as a way of dissipating feelings of emptiness and loneliness. She would engage saleswomen in expensive clothing stores in a form of theater. The patient directed a scene in which she would try on clothes and the saleswoman would tell her, in a maternal way, how pretty she looked.

In the eighth year of the analysis, Ms N began a session by telling me a dream: "I was in a department store that felt cavernous. A tinny voice from the speaker system was giving orders not only to the staff, but also to the customers. There were so many things I wanted to buy. There was a pair of lovely diamond earrings that were displayed in a soft satin-lined box – they looked like two tiny eggs in a bird's nest. I managed to get out of the store without buying anything."

My first impulse was to react to the dream as still another of the patient's attempts to get me to say my lines, or failing that, to elicit anger-tinged interpretations from me. But there was something subtly different about the dream and the way the patient told it to me. It felt to me that in the middle of a compulsive repetition of an all too familiar pattern of relatedness, something else obtruded when Ms N described the earrings. Her voice became less sing-song in tone and her speech slowed as if gently placing the two tiny eggs in the bird's nest. And then, as if that moment of softness had never occurred, Ms N, in a triumphant manner, "completed" the telling of the dream: "I managed to get out of the store without buying anything." It seemed to me that in this final comment, there was a pull for me to congratulate the patient on her accomplishment. At the same time, at a more unconscious level, her last statement had the effect of an announcement of her absolute control over the analytic situation, a control that would ensure that she would leave my consulting room no different from the person she was when she entered (having "managed to get out without buying anything").

In the few moments during and just after Ms N's telling me the dream, I was reminded of having gone shopping with my closest friend, J, a few years after we had graduated from college. The two of us were looking for an engagement ring for him to give to the woman with whom he was living. Neither of us knew the first thing about diamonds – or any other kind of jewelry. This "shopping experience" was one filled with feelings of warmth and closeness, but at the same time I was aware that there was a way in which I was participating in an event (the process of J's getting married) that I feared would change (or maybe even bring to an end) the friendship as it had existed to that point.

Quite unexpectedly, I found myself asking Ms N, "Why didn't you buy the earrings that you genuinely found so beautiful?" It took me a few moments to realize that I was speaking in a way that treated her dream as an actual event in the world of external reality. I could hear in my voice that I was not reacting to the provocative aspect of the patient's dream with anger of my own. My question was surprising in still another sense: the things that the patient had bought in the past had never held any symbolic meaning or aesthetic value for her – they were mere props in a transference–countertransference drama enacted with saleswomen and with me.

The combination of my responding to the dream as an actual event, and the sound of my voice as I asked Ms N why she had not bought the earrings, was not lost to the patient. She paused for almost a minute – which in itself was highly unusual for her – and then responded (as if the dream were an actual event) by saying, "I don't know. The idea never occurred to me."

Ms N's long-standing refusal/inability to make use of virtually everything I had to say might be thought of as her use of a form of pathological containing. The "script" from which I was to read my lines (while she directed the play) was the opposite of a kind of thinking that facilitates unconscious psychological work. Nothing original could come of it; no new thought could be generated. Her pathological containing function to that point had consisted primarily of a

106

form of "dreaming" in which the patient unconsciously denuded herself of human qualities (which she experienced as frailties) such as appetite for food, sexual desire and the need for genuine emotional relatedness to other people.

In the dream, the pathological containing function had become the contained – the "tinny" (inhuman) voice from the mechanical "speaker system" that ordered everyone around. My first impulse had been reflexively to respond to Ms N's dream as if it were no different from any of a hundred other instances in which she had told me a dream that was not a dream. However, the patient's tone of voice in telling me the portion of her dream involving the earrings, as well as the content of the imagery of that part of the dream, reflected the fact that she was beginning to be able to contain (i.e. to genuinely dream her emotional experience) which facilitated my own capacity for preconscious waking dreaming (reverie).

My reverie of shopping with J for an engagement ring served as a new form of containing that was not hostile to the contained, i.e., to the patient as I was experiencing her. My reverie experience, which involved feelings of affection, jealousy and fear of loss, might be thought of as a form of my participating in the dreaming of the patient's undreamt dream (Ogden, 2004b), i.e., my participating in her dreaming her experience in a non-dehumanizing way.

My reverie had issued in my asking a question in an unplanned way: "Why didn't you buy the earrings that you genuinely found so beautiful?" This question reflected the fact that I had not simply participated in dreaming the patient's formerly undreamable experience, I had momentarily become a figure in the dream that the two of us were dreaming in the session. In addition, the tone of voice with which I spoke to Ms N conveyed the fact that a change had taken place in my own way of experiencing (containing) the patient's emotional state. The words that I spontaneously spoke were quite the opposite of a set of "lines" (empty words) that had been extracted from me. Consequently, they could be given to her. (One cannot give something to someone who is trying to steal the very thing that one would like to give.) It seems to me in retrospect that my "asking/popping the question" reflected the fact that I was unconsciously, for the first time, able to dream (contain) the germ of a loving Oedipal transference–countertransference experience with the patient.

What I gave to Ms N in asking the question, consisted of my recognizing that her dreaming was of a new sort: interred in the familiar, unthinking provocation, there was a moment in which Ms N was actually beginning to engage in authentic unconscious psychological work. That work involved an unconscious fantasy of the two of us having beautiful (beloved) babies (the baby birds in the nest) who would be treated with the greatest tenderness and care. (Only in writing this paper did I realize that in the course of Ms N's telling me her dream, "tinny" had become "tiny.") My response to (containing of) the dream as reflected in my question served to convey a feeling that it may no longer be as necessary for the patient to reflexively dehumanize her emergent, still very fragile feelings of love for me.

III Concluding comments

At its core, Winnicott's holding is a conception of the mother's/analyst's role in safeguarding the continuity of the infant's or child's experience of being and becoming over time. Psychological development is a process in which the infant or child increasingly takes on the mother's function of maintaining the continuity of his experience of being alive. Maturation, from this perspective, entails the development of the infant's or child's capacity to generate and maintain for himself a sense of the continuity of his being over time – time that increasingly reflects a rhythm that is experienced by the infant or child as outside of his control. Common to all forms of holding of the continuity of one's being in time is the sensation-based emotional state of being gently, sturdily wrapped in the arms of the mother. In health, that physical/psychological core of holding remains a constant throughout one's life.

In contrast, Bion's container–contained at every turn involves a dynamic emotional interaction between dream-thoughts (the contained) and the capacity for dreaming (the container). Container and contained are fiercely, muscularly in tension with one another, coexisting in an uneasy state of mutual dependence.

Winnicott's holding and Bion's container–contained represent different analytic vertices from which to view the same analytic experience. Holding is concerned primarily with being and its relationship to time; the container–contained is centrally concerned with the processing (dreaming) of thoughts derived from lived emotional experience. Together they afford "stereoscopic" depth to the understanding of the emotional experiences that occur in the analytic setting.

8

On psychoanalytic writing

For more than thirty years analytic writing has been one of life's pleasures for me. It would be of great satisfaction to be able to provide the reader a glimpse into the nature of that experience and something of what I have learned from it. I will begin by delineating what, for me, is essential to the literary genre of analytic writing. Having done that, I will look closely at the way the language works in a passage taken from my own clinical writing and one taken from Winnicott's theoretical writing. Finally, I will offer a series of reflections on analytic writing – some personal to my own way of going about writing, others pertaining to what I believe to be true of all good analytic writing.

I The genre of analytic writing

Analytic writing is a literary genre that involves the conjunction of an interpretation and a work of art. I think of this form of writing as a conversation between an original analytic idea (developed in a scholarly manner) and the creation in words of something like an analytic experience. Every analytic idea is an interpretation in that it directly or indirectly addresses the relationship between conscious and unconscious experience, and thus constitutes an interpretation in an analytic sense. At the same time, analytic writing necessarily involves the making of a work of art as the writer must use language in an artful way if he is to create for the reader *in the experience of reading* a sense not only of the critical elements of an analytic experience that the writer has had with a patient, but also "the music of what happen[ed]" (Heaney, 1979, p.173) in that experience (i.e. what it felt like to be there in the experience). (Bion, 1978, seems to have had something similar in mind when he said, "If we want to make a scientific communication, we shall also have to make a work of art" [p. 195]. He did not elaborate on this idea.)

The analytic writer is continually contending with the reality that an analytic experience – like all other experiences – does not come to us in words. An experience cannot be told or written; an experience is what it is. One can no more say or write an analytic experience than one can say or write the aroma of coffee or the taste of chocolate (Ogden, 2003b). When a patient tells a dream from the previous night, he is not telling the dream itself; rather, he is making a new verbally symbolized experience in the act of (seemingly) telling the visually symbolized experience from the previous night. Similarly, when we read an analyst's written account of an experience with a patient, what we are reading is not the experience itself, but the writer's creation of a new (literary) experience while (seemingly) writing the experience that he had with the analysand. As Bion put it,

> I cannot have as much confidence in my ability to tell the reader what has happened as I have in my ability to do something to the reader [in the experience of reading] that I have had done to me. I have had an emotional experience [with a patient]; I feel confident in my ability to recreate that emotional experience [in the reader's experience of reading], but not to represent it.

> (1992, p. 219)

In creating for the reader, in the experience of reading, something like his experience that he had with the analysand, the analytic writer finds himself conscripted into the ranks of imaginative writers. However, unlike writers of fiction, poetry or drama, a person writing in the analytic genre must remain faithful to the fundamental structure of what actually occurred between himself and the patient (as he experienced it). The analytic writer is continually bumping up against a paradoxical truth: analytic experience (which cannot be said or written) must be transformed into "fiction" (an imaginative rendering of an experience in words), if what is true to the experience is to be conveyed to the reader. In other words, analytic writing, in conveying what is true to an analytic experience, "turns facts into fictions. It is only when facts become fictions [that] . . . they become real [in the experience of reading]" (Weinstein, 1998). At the same time, the "fiction" that is created in words must reflect the reality of what occurred. The experience of that reality remains alive in the analytic writer not only in the form of memory but, as important, in the way he has been changed by and continues to be changed by it.

While engaged in analytic writing, I am all the time moving back and forth between the analytic experience that remains alive in me and the "characters" I am creating in the writing. There is a distinctive form of psychological/literary work involved in creating and maintaining a living connection between the actual people (the patient and analyst) and the "characters" in the written story, and between the flow of the lived experience and the unfolding written "storyline."

The characters in the story depend for their lives on the real people (the patient and analyst); and bringing to life what happened between these people in the analytic setting depends on the vitality and three-dimensionality of the characters created in the story. The writer's keeping alive his connection with both his lived experience with the patient and his experience with the characters in the story entails a delicate balancing act. The actual people and the characters are continually in danger of flying off in different directions. When that happens, all the life drains from the story; the characters are no longer believable; what they say feels contrived. It is in the feat of sustaining a vital conversation between the lived analytic experience and the life of the written story that the art of psychoanalytic writing resides.

II An experience in clinical writing

I shall now look closely at a short clinical passage taken from one of my recent papers (Chapter 1 of this volume) in an effort to convey something of the conscious and unconscious thought process that went into the writing. The passage that I will discuss is the opening paragraph of a detailed presentation of an experience in analysis.

> A few days after Mr A and I had set a time to meet for an initial consultation, his secretary called to cancel the meeting for vague reasons having to do with Mr A's business commitments. He called me several weeks later to apologize for the cancellation and to ask to arrange another meeting. In our first session, Mr A, a man in his mid-40s, told me that he had wanted to begin analysis for some time (his wife was currently in analysis), but he had kept putting it off. He quickly added (as if responding to the expectable "therapeutic" question), "I don't know why I was afraid of analysis." He went on, "Although my life looks very good from the outside – I'm successful at my work, I have a very good marriage and three children whom I dearly love – I feel almost all the time that something is terribly wrong." [Mr A's use of the phrases "afraid of analysis," "dearly love," and "terribly wrong," felt to me like anxious unconscious efforts to feign candor while, in fact, telling me almost nothing.] I said to Mr A that his having asked his secretary to speak for him made me think that he may feel that his own voice and his own words somehow fail him. Mr A looked at me as if I were crazy and said, "No, my cell phone wasn't working and rather than pay the outrageous amounts that hotels charge for phone calls, I e-mailed my secretary telling her to call you."
>
> (Ogden, 2004b, p. 868)

Deciding how and where to begin a case description is no small matter. The opening of a clinical account, when it works, has all the feel of the inevitable. It leads the reader to feel: how else would one begin to tell this story? The place where one starts, in addition to providing an important structural element to the story and to the paper as a whole, makes a significant implicit statement about the writer's way of thinking, the sorts of things he notices and values, and, in particular, which of the infinite number of junctures in this human experience deserves pride of place in the telling of the story.

In the opening paragraph being discussed, even before the appearance of the subject of the first sentence, there is an introductory clause – "A few days after Mr A and I set a time to meet for an initial consultation" – that unobtrusively signals what is to happen in the clinical account as a whole. A promise is made (the agreement to meet at a given time and place for a particular purpose) which, in the next part of the sentence, the patient breaks. My experience with Mr A is turned into an experience in reading in part by means of structuring the opening sentence in this way. The story of Mr A's analysis that is beginning to be told is a story of broken (unspoken) promises: the patient's betrayal of the trust of his younger sister while they were "playing doctor," the patient's betrayal of himself by not facing up to what he had done to his sister, and his mother's breaking of an implicit promise that she would genuinely be his mother.

The subject of the opening sentence is neither Mr A nor I, but Mr A's secretary: "his secretary called to cancel the meeting. . . ." On the face of it, this is an odd choice, but in giving her the opening lines (in conveying the patient's message to me), the sentence is showing (as opposed to saying) an absence – the absence of the patient. The patient, in speaking through the secretary, is speaking from a psychological place defined by his absence. Even though the patient did not attend the first session of his analysis – the cancelled session – the session nonetheless took place in my mind and, I presume, in his. It was a session in which the patient was present in the form of his absence from his analysis and (I suspected) from many other parts of his life.

The theme of deception appears in the opening sentence in the form of Mr A's explanation for the cancellation, which I characterize as consisting of "vague reasons having to do with Mr A's business commitments." Neither the reader nor I (as character) know the nature of Mr A's business at this point in the story. By referring to Mr A's "business" before its nature is revealed, there is a faint suggestion that his unnamed business may be illegitimate or a cover for something else. Also dimly flickering in this sentence is the suggestion that Mr A may be involved in deceiving himself by rationalizing his absence from the first session of his analysis. This layering of possibilities – some manifest, others only barely perceptible – generates an ominous sense of vaguely destructive forces at work, a whiff of the patient's subterranean life.

While the opening sentence may work in the ways I have suggested, I do not mean to say that I consciously constructed the sentence with these ends in mind. The sentence "came to me" in the act of writing as a dream comes unbidden

112

in sleep. In an early draft, the story began with my meeting Mr A in the waiting room where he addressed me by my first name. As disquieting as that event had been, I deleted it from the story because I felt that the effect created by the sentence I have been discussing was more richly layered (and hence more interesting). Moving that sentence from the third paragraph of the original version to the position of opening sentence allowed it to take on more dramatic force – thus creating in the writing something of the emotional impact that Mr A had had on me at the very beginning of his analysis. Only after making this sentence the opening sentence of the story did I recognize that it contained in germinal form the entirety of the story that would follow.

As in the writing process that I have just described, I find that it is important not to know the shape of the story from the start, but to allow it to take form in the process of writing it. Not knowing the end of the story while at the beginning preserves for the writer as well as for the reader a sense of the utter unpredictability of every life experience: we never know what is going to happen before it happens. The equivalent in writing is to allow the piece "to tell how it can . . . It finds its own name as it goes" (Frost, 1939, p.777).

In the penultimate sentence of the paragraph being discussed, I (as character) speak for the first time in response to what has happened to this point in the story: "I said to Mr A that his having asked his secretary to speak for him made me think that he may feel that his own voice and his own words somehow fail him." What I say begins to define for Mr A and for the reader how I conceive of psychoanalysis. My verbal response to Mr A was, to my mind, psychoanalytic in the sense that it constituted a verbally symbolized interpretation of what I believed to be the leading anxiety in the transference. In addition, it had something of the quality of "an interpretation in action" (Ogden, 1994b) in that the stance I was taking in making the interpretation reflected an active refusal on my part to allow the patient's angry and fearfully evasive introduction of himself – the way he handled the initial (cancelled) session – to remain an unnoticed, unspoken event. My act of framing those actions was significant not only as an effort to begin to understand the meanings of what was happening; as important, it served as a way of showing – not explaining to – the patient (and the reader) what it means to enter into a psychoanalytic relationship. Psychoanalysis is an experience in which the analyst takes the patient seriously, in part by treating everything that he says and does as potentially meaningful communications to the analyst (Ogden, 1989). In the instance being discussed, the actions Mr A took in connection with the initial meeting constituted his first communications concerning what he (unconsciously) felt I should know about him if I was to be of help to him. My response constituted an action in its own right that was meant to capture the patient's attention (and imagination). The interpretation had a crispness to it that is there in the sensory feel of the written sentence: There is an abrupt drop from the conscious, descriptive level ("his having asked his secretary to speak for him") to the preconscious-unconscious level ("he may feel that his own voice and his own words somehow fail him").

The specific words I use in writing the dialogue in the final sentences of the opening paragraph are of great importance to my effort to bring to life in the writing my experience with Mr A. I had not taken notes during the session so the dialogue for this scene required that I find words that both capture the essence of what the patient and I actually said as well as the voice with which we each spoke.[1] Even though what I said is not put in quotation marks, the sentence nonetheless conveys a sense of the voice in which I made the inter-pretation. It was a voice that surprised the patient (which can be heard in his response). The dialogue also reflects the way in which the patient noticed that he was encountering in this initial exchange not just a new person, but a new way of thinking and speaking. The voice with which I spoke was direct and eschewed conventional rules of etiquette (as well as the patriarchal tones of the traditional way a doctor talks to a patient). The voice is not arrogant, nor does it claim omniscience, but it is the voice of someone who believes he has some familiarity with a level of human relatedness that is new and more than a little frightening to the patient.

Mr A did not say what frightened him about beginning analysis, but his fear was palpably present in his response to what I said: "My cell phone wasn't work-ing and rather than pay the outrageous amounts that hotels charge for phone calls, I e-mailed my secretary telling her to call you." In this portion of the session, Mr A was expressing a great many feelings at once. My task as a writer is to use words in a way that somehow captures that simultaneity. The words "Mr A looked at me as if I were crazy" serve to express (with mild irony) the patient's angry, fearful rebellion against the way I framed the events surround-ing his secretary's calling me. In his protest, he invokes common sense in defense not only of his perspective, but also of his sanity.[2] (My use of the word "crazy" in describing how Mr A looked at me is intended to suggest his fear of the psychotic aspect of himself.)

In writing each element of the patient's response, the language I use is meant to convey a sense of the pressure of the unconscious almost bursting through the spoken words: "My cell phone wasn't working" – i.e., he felt blocked by my interpretation from speaking and thinking in the way in which he was accustomed. "Rather than pay the outrageous amounts hotels charge for phone calls" – i.e., he felt powerless in the analytic setting where I make self-serving rules which he feared would not take into account who he is and what he needs. "I e-mailed my secretary telling her to call you [to cancel the meeting]" – i.e., he refused to submit to me and my ways of thinking and speaking which he feared I was attempting to impose on him; he could more safely communicate without speaking (through the use of e-mail and his secretary's speaking for him); he could try to protect himself against my power (and the power of his own warded-off thoughts and feelings) by the use of self-deception and evasiveness (in canceling the first session). In the words I use to express my sense of Mr A's emotional experience, I am attempting to create a voice for him in which the reader can hear the simultaneity of a frightened child's pleading, a bully's painful insecurity and hollow bravado, and a man in psychological distress who is covertly asking for help. Each reader will determine for himself whether these lines succeed in bringing an analytic experience to life in the experience of reading.

III "The profoundest thinking that we have" in theoretical analytic writing

Though an analytic writer cannot say an experience, he can say what an experience was like. Consequently, he is at every turn in the business of making metaphors, "not pretty metaphors . . . [but] the profoundest thinking that we have" (Frost, 1930, p. 719). A skillful writer uses language in a way that is so subtle that very often the reader is only subliminally aware that the use of metaphor is the predominant medium in which meaning is being conveyed. Winnicott is masterful in this regard as he describes the child's possible responses to his mother's absence while she is away having a baby:

> When no understanding can be given [to a very young child regarding the impending birth of a sibling], then when the mother is away to have a new baby she is dead from the point of view of the child. This is what dead means.
>
> It is a matter of days or hours or minutes. Before the limit is reached the mother is still alive; after this limit is overstepped she is dead. In between is a precious moment of anger, but this is quickly lost or perhaps never experienced, always potential and carrying fear of violence.
>
> (Winnicott, 1971b, pp. 21–22)

In these very plainly worded sentences, metaphors are quietly residing within other metaphors. Winnicott's apparently simple statement, "This is what dead means" (composed of five monosyllabic words) is dense with meaning. This sentence is subtly ambiguous: Who has died? – Is it the mother or the child? The ambiguity allows it to be both at the same time. The child's experience of "what dead means" is not only an experience of the mother's being absolutely unresponsive (metaphorically dead) to the child (in her absence); it is also an experience of the child's being metaphorically dead/unresponsive to himself, dead to the pain of the mother's absence. Though the former (the mother's absolute unresponsiveness to the child in her absence) is what the metaphor apparently refers to, the latter (the child's deadness to himself) is the more quietly forceful image and the more psychologically destructive aspect of the emotional experience.

115

Winnicott continues: "It is a matter of days or hours or minutes. [What is a matter of days or hours or minutes? The reader momentarily lives with the child's confusion about what is happening.] Before the limit is reached the mother is still alive; after this limit is overstepped she is dead [and the child is dead]." Here, Winnicott is constructing a metaphor of a line separating the land of the living (mother and child) and the land of the dead (mother and child).

The metaphor is then expanded: "In between is a precious moment of anger." There is a space between the land of the living and the land of the dead, a space in which there is "a precious moment of anger". The ambiguity of "This is what dead means" elaborates itself here. There is a (metaphoric) space opening in which something other than the death of the child might occur. "A precious moment of anger" is established as the opposite of the metaphorical death of the child (and secondarily that of the mother). The words "precious" and "anger" collide in the phrase "precious moment of anger." From this collision (both in the experience of the child and in the experience of reading), there emerges a momentary, fragile union of vitality and destructiveness. It is a moment that "is quickly lost or perhaps never experienced, always potential and carrying fear of violence."

What "dead means" is developed still further: Dead means the child's loss of (or never experiencing) the aliveness to be had in feeling his anger as his own; it also means the loss of the durability of his sense of self in the experience of sustaining his anger over time. His fear that his anger will turn into actual violence which will damage or destroy his mother poses a constant threat to his ability to remain alive to himself in his anger. The phrase "carrying fear of violence" is without a human subject – the subject is "moment" – thus conveying a sense of the way in which this fear of violence is not experienced by the child as his own creation, his own feeling. Rather, it is an impersonal force by which the child feels inhabited and over which he feels he has no control. Destroying himself, his capacity to feel anything may be preferable to the risk of killing his mother as a consequence of the violence with which he is occupied.

In these five sentences, Winnicott takes a rather ordinary metaphor in which the mother's absence feels like her death and transforms it first into a metaphor subtly suggesting the death of the child in the face of the absence of the mother; and then into a metaphor in which a fragile space in which the child's state of emotional aliveness is sustained by "precious" anger; and finally the metaphor is completed by incorporating the idea that the fragile emotional vitality of the child (which resides in the collision of the precious and the violent) may be extinguished by the child himself if he believes that his own vitality (in his experience of anger) poses great threat to the life of his mother.

As can be seen, metaphor ("the profoundest thinking that we have"), when used skillfully, allows theoretical analytic writing to mean much more than it is able to say.

IV Reflections on analytic writing

In this final section, I will offer some observations on writing in the analytic genre. Since writing is a unitary event, breaking it into parts creates an artificial, kaleidoscopic effect. The more that the different facets are viewed as qualities of a whole, the closer the reader will come to gaining a sense of how I have come to view and experience the writing process. Some of the entries that follow are quite brief, others much longer – I have tried to say only what I feel needs to be said concerning a given aspect of writing, and then to move on.

A good many of my reflections on how I write reflect ways of going about writing that are idiosyncratic to me. These ways of approaching writing should not be viewed as prescriptions for the way analytic writing ought to be done. Each author must develop over time his own methods for engaging in analytic writing. By contrast, other of my reflections on writing address what I believe to be attributes of all good analytic writing.

"After all, writing is nothing more than a guided dream"
(Borges, 1970b, p. 13)

While the art of writing may be guided dreaming, it is important not to romanticize the process by viewing it as a gift from one's muse, a state of being passively entranced. Writing is hard work. Learning to guide one's dreaming involves a lifetime of reading and writing. I have never been able to write an analytic article in fewer than several hundred hours. The time needed for writing must be created – it is not simply there asking to be used for writing. I write very early in the morning. I do so not with a feeling of being burdened by the work of writing, but with a sense of excitement (and anxiety) about what may happen that morning in the experience of writing. Often during those early morning hours of writing, I have had the thought that there is nothing in the world that I would rather be doing at that moment.

A meditation and a wrestling match

Analytic writing is, for me, comprised of equal parts meditation and the experience of wrestling a beast to the ground. As a meditation, writing constitutes a way of being with myself and of hearing myself coming into being in a way that has no equivalent in any other sector of my life. This "state of writing" is very similar to my experience of reverie in the analytic setting. When in a "state of writing," I am in a heightened state of receptivity to unconscious experience, while at the same time, bringing to bear on the experience an ear for how I may be able to make literary use of what I am thinking and feeling.

117

The state of writing is a very physical experience in which my thinking is far more auditory than are most other forms of thinking. I often say the words aloud as I write, never being certain which ones I have actually spoken and which I have merely thought. I try out a phrase, reject it, try another, return to the first, scribbling and scratching out, linking isolated clauses with arrows, ending up with a palimpsest of words and ideas.

Like the analytic reverie state, the state of writing is a form of waking dreaming, an experience of living at "the frontier of dreaming" (Ogden, 2001b). When a writer is in such a psychological state, language itself feels infused with the color and intensity of the unconscious. When I attempt to write at times when I am not able to live at the frontier of dreaming – for example, when I am tired or preoccupied – my writing may be coherent, even forceful in its logic, but it lacks a pulse.

At the same time, writing is a very muscular activity in which the writer enters into a battle with language. Language, as if of its own accord, resists being tamed and pressed into the service of expressing inherently wordless experience. Conrad observed that words are "the great foes of reality" (quoted by Pritchard, 1991, p. 128).

"A writer writes"
(from the film Throw Momma From the Train [1987])

As I view it, there is no such thing as a potential writer. When one is writing or composing in one's mind, one is a writer. When I am not writing or composing, I feel that I am someone who used to be a writer. Once the process of writing begins I am in it, possessed by it night and day. Everything I hear, see, read and imagine informs, shapes, modifies my writing. The writing is dreaming me into existence as much as I am dreaming the writing into existence. It is not an altogether pleasurable state in which to be; there is a quality of having lost control of one's mind. In a sense one has lost one's mind. Part of becoming a writer is developing a way of living in that state while going about the rest of one's life (e.g. being a spouse, a parent, an analyst, a friend and so on). It is also necessary for a writer to be forgiving of himself for the atrocious stuff with which he fills so many pages. Without such self-acceptance, writing is too punishing to sustain.

The author disappears leaving traces

A writer learns in the course of becoming a writer how to get out of his own way and out of the reader's way. Shakespeare's genius lay in his ability to dis-appear from the space between the reader and the writer, between the audience and the play. Borges (1949) in a parable describes Shakespeare as a man with "no one in him" (p. 248) and his life as "a dream dreamt by no one" (p. 248).

> History adds that before or after dying he found himself in the presence of God and told Him: "I who have been so many men in vain want to be one and myself." The voice of the Lord answered from a whirlwind: "Neither am I anyone; I have dreamt the world as you dreamt your work, my Shakespeare, and among the forms in my dream are you, who like myself are many and no one."
>
> (p. 249)

Getting in one's own way in writing may take the form of an infatuation with one's cleverness or one's facility with words; or it may involve the use of writing as a confessional or as an opportunity for self-aggrandizement. The subject of such writing is the author himself, not the subject matter being discussed. "To write is not to be absent but to become absent; to be someone and then go away, leaving traces" (Wood, 1994, p. 18).

> *"I try to leave out the parts that people skip"*
> *(Elmore Leonard, 1991, p. 32)*

Good analytic writing is sparse and unassuming – just the essentials, not an extra word or repeated idea. Consequently, good writing is almost impossible to paraphrase – to condense it is to leave out something essential to its meaning. "For where there is amenability to paraphrase, there the sheets have never been rumpled, there poetry, so to speak, has never spent the night" (Mandelstam, 1933, p. 252).

> *"Some kind of . . . [literary] form has to be found or I'll go crazy"*
> *(William Carlos Williams, 1932, p. 129)*

The form or structure of an analytic paper may be the most original and innovative of its qualities. Creating a literary form for an article may also be one of the most difficult parts of the work of analytic writing. Writing an analytic paper involves a prodigious act of coordination in which the parts are continually in the process of generating the whole. At its best, form "virtually emerges out of itself" (Mandelstam, 1933, p. 261). The structure of a paper vitalizes the ideas and emotional experiences that the writer (together with the reader) are creating and developing.

There is a strong tendency in analytic writing to consider the form (if it is considered at all) as given. There is a standard form: a paper begins with the presentation of an idea; there then follows a review of the literature; one or more clinical illustrations are offered; and the paper concludes with an elaboration of the original idea. This is an important form that analytic writers must master just as artists begin by learning the classical forms and techniques that are fundamental to their art, whether the art be painting, music, poetry or dance. But, since form and content are inseparable, in the course of one's development as a writer, one must begin to experiment with developing original forms for giving shape to one's ideas.

A good deal of Freud's genius as a writer resides in the arena of literary forms. He invented one form after the other ranging from the humorous conceit of lectures being delivered to an audience of skeptics in his *Introductory Lectures on Psycho-Analysis* (1916–1917); to the form of casual conversation with colleagues in his "Papers on Technique" (1911–1915); to the multiple openings and multiple endings of the "Wolf Man" case (1918); to the careful construction of a "scientific" argument in *The Interpretation of Dreams* (1900). It is interesting to note with regard to form, that the first chapter of *The Interpretation of Dreams* is an exhaustive 95-page review of the history of writing on dreams. Freud summarizes practically every previous theory of dreams and finds that each is valid; but each captures only one facet of the truth at the expense of the others. His own theory of dreams does not refute the others; rather, it encompasses them all.

In my own recent papers, I have experimented with form. One of those papers, "On not being able to dream" (Ogden, 2003a; Chapter 4), is structured by the juxtaposition of three renderings – each in a different medium – of the experience of not being able to dream. The three media in which the experience is rendered are those of an idea, a story and an analytic experience. The idea is an elaboration and extension of Bion's concept of dreaming and of not being able to dream; the story is a Borges fiction in which a character acquires infinite memory, but at the same time, loses his ability to sleep and to dream; and the analytic experience involves work with a patient in which she and I develop the capacity to dream together in the course of the analysis. The form of this paper is intended to generate a living process in the experience of reading in which the three renderings talk to one another in a way that mirrors the living conversation with ourselves that constitutes dreaming. (It also mirrors a conversation among three forms of human expression that are of great importance to me: psychoanalytic theory, literature and analytic practice.)

In another paper, "An introduction to the reading of Bion" (Ogden, 2004a; Chapter 6), I experiment with form by using the differences between the experience of reading Bion's early work and that of reading his late work as paradigmatic of the differences between the way Bion thinks in these two periods of writing. In this way I incorporate into the structure of the paper what I believe to be the most important aspect of Bion's contribution to psychoanalysis: the exploration of *how* we think and dream, *how* we process experience (as opposed to *what* we think, e.g. the content of unconscious fantasies).

In still another paper, "This art of psychoanalysis: Dreaming undreamt dreams and interrupted cries" (Ogden, 2004b; Chapter 1), I attempt to state in two paragraphs the essence of the analytic process ("Granted, . . . the undertaking was impossible from the very beginning" [Borges, 1941b, p. 40]). In using this form, I am drawing on the power of the concentration of words to generate an expansion of meaning (which is the hallmark of poetry [Stoppard, 1999]). I go on to "unpack" that highly condensed statement clause by clause, sentence by sentence as one might do in closely reading a poem. I then illustrate my thinking with a clinical account (the opening paragraph of which I discussed in detail earlier in this chapter).

Whether or not my experiments in form succeed as literary inventions is very much open to question. What, for me, is certain is the idea that experimenting with the literary form used in analytic writing is part and parcel of the effort to develop fresh ways of thinking analytically. A fresh idea demands a fresh form in which to say it. Freud's clinical work that he presented in his case studies could not have been communicated in the forms available in the medical writings of his time.

The bullshit detector and Menard's Quixote

Each writer has his own writing habits. Mine include writing a first draft with pen and pad; I have never been able to compose while typing. For me, there is an unintended, yet highly valuable consequence of writing by hand: I have no choice (given my typing skills) but to dictate the manuscript when my notebook pages have become so crammed with crossed out and inserted words and sentences that I am hardly able to read what I have written. This method – writing by hand and dictating – has forced me to read aloud what I have written. In my experience there is no better bullshit detector. Reading one's writing aloud rousts out of hiding language that is pretentious or self-satisfied; repetitive or wordy; excessively clever or dismally ponderous; diminished by jargon and cliché; imitative of others or a recycled version of one's own previous writings; soporific on account of unvarying sentence structure or off-putting as a consequence of exhibiting how "literary" one is.

Perhaps most important, reading aloud what I have written provides me with a response to the question: am I offering an original perspective on a significant psychoanalytic matter? I believe that there is nothing new under the sun but that it is always possible to view something old in a fresh and original way (Ogden, 2003b). No writer, to my mind, need worry that what he has to say has already been said. Of course, it has previously been said innumerable times, but it never has been said from the perspective that each of us might bring to it if we dare to try.

When an analytic writer for whom I am serving as a consultant protests that he has discovered that many others have already exhausted the topic he has in mind to explore, I am reminded of Borges's (1941b) story "Pierre Menard, author of the *Quixote*." Borges's fictional late-nineteenth century novelist, Pierre Menard, set out to write the *Quixote* – not a memorized transcription of it, or a modern version of it, or additional chapters for it, but the *Quixote* itself. He succeeded in writing two chapters of the book from which Borges quotes a few lines and juxtaposes them with the corresponding lines from Cervantes' *Quixote*. The reader sees with his own eyes that the two sets of lines are identical, word for word, comma for comma. And yet Borges finds Menard's *Quixote* far superior to Cervantes' : Menard's text, written by a nineteenth-century man, is admirably free of "local color," i.e., free of window dressing composed of detailed depictions of sixteenth-century Spanish life. Cervantes achieved nothing in omitting those descriptive ornaments because his sixteenth-century audience was of course familiar with the circumstances of their lives and customs. For Menard, a nineteenth-century writer, to leave them out is genius.

For the mid- to late-twentieth-century analytic writer, it is genius to freshly (re)discover transference (in the total situation [Joseph, 1985]); to arrive freshly at the concept of the body ego (in the notion of the unity of the psyche-soma in health [Winnicott, 1949]); to come upon, as if for the first time, the concept of dream-work (conceived of as a process in which conscious lived experience is made available to the unconscious for psychological work [Bion, 1962a]), and on and on.

The dark night of the soul of the analytic writer

There are two junctures in the writing process that for me are most difficult and most emotionally draining. The first involves arriving at an idea that captures my imagination and then finding a way to develop it. Most often I begin by stating the idea as plainly as I can in the space of a paragraph or two. I then write twenty to twenty-five handwritten pages of whatever comes to mind in relation to the idea I am trying out. If there is a single paragraph that seems promising in these pages, I am very pleased. If there are three or four paragraphs, I am elated. Often the ideas in these successful paragraphs have only a tangential relationship to the idea with which I began. I then write a new opening statement for the paper using the ideas and some of the language for these ideas contained in the initial draft.

I write anywhere from five to ten drafts (major re-workings of the structure and primary themes) and easily fifty re-workings of a great many individual words, phrases and sentences. After each draft, the opening statement concerning the subject of the paper has to be revised.

The second of the two junctures in the writing process that I find most trying is reading the manuscript after it has been transcribed from my dictation. It has never once occurred on reading the first typed version of the paper that I have not felt profoundly disappointed and discouraged. Many of the sentences and paragraphs seem like little more than thin disguises for a lack of depth of thought. Carrying on with the writing of the paper at this stage is most of all a process of stating more clearly for myself the subject matter I am trying to address. The kernel of an idea is there, but it is so mired in verbiage that it is difficult to detect. The craft of finding that kernel involves ruthlessly cutting unnecessary sentences, paragraphs and entire sections of the paper.

It is has been my experience that what happens at this point in the writing process makes or breaks a piece of writing. If I succeed in turning this corner, it is as if I have arrived at a clearance in which I can think with a clarity that I have not experienced to this point in the writing process. Phrases come to mind that capture essences that, to this point, have been barely discernible. It is at this stage of writing that I imagine that Winnicott (1956) came upon the phrase "going on being" (p. 303), and Bion (1962a) wrote, "The patient who cannot dream cannot got to sleep and cannot wake up" (p. 7), and Balint (1968) found the phrase "harmonious interpenetrating mix-up" (p. 136), and Loewald (1960) wrote "ghosts of the unconscious are laid . . . to rest as ancestors" (p. 249). In reading such phrases and sentences in context, it is unmistakable to the ear of the writer and of the reader that the idea could not be stated in any other way; any other words would convey something substantially different. It is here that a substantial part of the grace of good analytic writing is born.

When analytic writing is good, it is evident that the author's intent has not been to be "poetic" (if it were, the sentences would feel embarrassingly con-trived). Rather, the words and phrases have unselfconscious poise. Even when most readers cannot hear the difference between a dashed off piece of writing and a piece arrived at by means of long hours of struggling with words, the writer himself can hear the difference, and there is nothing that matters more to a writer.

Notes

Chapter 1

1   Any effort to describe psychoanalysis necessarily draws upon the reader's experience of psychoanalysis. One could write volumes on the subject of dogs, but unless the reader has experienced a living dog, he will not know what a dog *is*. A dog *is* a dog; psychoanalysis *is* psychoanalysis; "the world, unfortunately, is real [unwaveringly itself]; I, unfortunately, am Borges" (Borges, 1946, p. 234).

2   Unlike nightmares, which occur in REM sleep (the sleep state in which most dreaming occurs), night terrors occur in deep, slow wave sleep (Hartmann, 1984). Although I make mention in this chapter of neurophysiological data associated with night terrors and nightmares (brain wave activity recorded in sleep studies), this data is of purely metaphorical value. The fact that brain wave activity associated with night terrors and with nightmares is different does not lend support to the idea that the psychoanalytic conception of night terrors and nightmares differs in analogous ways. The neurophysiologic findings of sleep researchers offer nothing more (and nothing less) than intriguing parallels between the activity of the brain and the experience of the mind, and potentially valuable metaphors for use in psychoanalytic thinking about dreaming, not being able to dream, and interrupted dreaming.

3   While both adults and children experience night terrors and nightmares, these phenomena are more prevalent in children; for the sake of clarity of exposition, I will speak of these phenomena in terms of the experience of a child.

4   Frost (1928) writes: "I have stood still and stopped the sound of feet/ When far away an interrupted cry/ Came over houses from another street" (p. 234). (See Ogden, 1999b, for a discussion of this poem.)

5   I include in the notion of reverie all of the meanderings of the psychesoma of the analyst including the most quotidian, unobtrusive, thoughts and feelings, ruminations and daydreams, bodily sensations, and so on, which usually feel utterly unrelated to what the patient is saying and doing at that moment. Reveries are not the product of the psychesoma of the analyst alone but of the combined unconscious of patient and analyst (Ogden, 1994a, 1994c, 1996, 1997a, 1997b, 1997c, 2001a). As will be shown in the clinical portion of this chapter, the analyst's reveries provide a form of indirect access to the unconscious life of the analytic relationship.

6   Central among the ideas that, for me, constitute a psychoanalytic perspective are a conception of the relationships among conscious, preconscious and unconscious aspects of mind; the concept of transference–countertransference; a conception of an internal object world; the idea of depressive, paranoid-schizoid and autistic-contiguous modes of generating experience and their associated forms of subjectivity, anxiety, defense, object-relatedness and psychological growth; the concepts of splitting, projective identification and manic defense; the notion of the human need for truth; a conception of psychological aliveness and deadness; the concept of a psychological space between reality and fantasy in which the individual may develop the capacity for thinking symbolically, thereby coming imaginatively to life; the idea of the analytic frame; an understanding of the pivotal role, from birth onward, of sexuality in healthy development and in psychopathology; a conception of the way in which the development of capacities for symbolization and self-awareness are inseparable from the development of internal and external object relationships (including maternal mirroring and oedipal triangulation).

7   The names we give to feelings – for example, feeling alone, feeling lonely, feeling frightened – are broad generic categories that do not say feelings any more than the word "chocolate" says an experience of tasting chocolate. One cannot possibly communicate in words the taste of chocolate to a person who has never tasted it. Tasting, like all other sensory and emotional experiences, cannot be said.

8   My reverie experience in the work with Mr A had been extremely sparse and difficult to utilize in the first year or so of the analysis.

Chapter 3

1   I use the term "object relations theory" to refer to a group of psychoanalytic theories holding in common a loosely knit set of metaphors that address the intrapsychic and interpersonal effects of relationships among unconscious "internal" objects (i.e., among unconscious split-off parts of the personality). This group of theories coexists in Freudian psychoanalytic theory as a whole with many other overlapping, complementary, often contradictory lines of thought (each utilizing somewhat different sets of metaphors).

2   I have previously discussed (Ogden, 2001c) the interdependence of the vitality of the ideas and the life of the writing in a very different, but no less significant psychoanalytic contribution: Winnicott's (1945) "Primitive emotional development."

3   I am using Strachey's 1957 translation of "Mourning and melancholia" in the *Standard Edition* as the text for my discussion. It is beyond the scope of this chapter to address questions relating to the quality of that translation.

4   Less than a year before writing "Mourning and melancholia," Freud (1914a) remarked that no one need wonder about his role in the history of psychoanalysis: "Psycho-analysis is my creation; for ten years I was the only person who concerned himself with it" (p. 7).

5   Freud's term "melancholia" is roughly synonymous with "depression" as the latter term is currently used.

6   Freud comments that "it never occurs to us to regard . . . [mourning] as a pathological condition and to refer it to medical treatment.. We rely on its being

overcome after a certain lapse of time, and we look upon any interference with it as useless or even harmful" (1917b, pp. 243–244). This observation is offered as a statement of the self-evident and may have been so in Vienna in 1915. But, to my mind, that understanding today is paid lip service far more often than it is genuinely honored.

7   While Freud made use of the idea of "an internal world" in "Mourning and melancholia," it was Klein (1935, 1940, 1952) who transformed the idea into a systematic theory of the structure of the unconscious and of the interplay between the internal object world and the world of external objects. In developing her conception of the unconscious, Klein richly contributed to a critical alteration of analytic theory. She shifted the dominant metaphors from those associated with Freud's topographic and structural models to a set of spatial metaphors (some stated, some only suggested in "Mourning and melancholia"). These spatial metaphors depict an unconscious inner world inhabited by "internal objects" – split-off aspects of the ego – that are bound together in "internal object relationships" by powerful affective ties. (For a discussion of the concepts of "internal objects" and "internal object relations" as these ideas evolved in the work of Freud, Abraham, Klein, Fairbairn and Winnicott, see Ogden, 1983.)

8   At the same time as the infant is engaged in the movement from narcissistic identification to narcissistic object-tie, he is simultaneously engaged in the development of a "type . . . of object-choice [driven by object-libido], which may be called the 'anaclitic' or 'attachment type'" (Freud, 1914b, p. 87). The latter form of object relatedness has its "source" (p. 87) in the infant's "original attachment . . . [to] the persons who are concerned with a child's feeding, care, and protection . . . " (p. 87). In health, the two forms of object relatedness – narcissistic and attachment-type – develop "side by side" (p. 87). Under less than optimal environmental or biological circumstances, the infant may develop psychopathology characterized by an almost exclusive reliance on narcissistic object relatedness (as opposed to relatedness of an attachment sort).

9   The reader can hear the voice of Melanie Klein (1935, 1940) in this part of Freud's comments on mania. All three elements of Klein's (1935) well-known clinical triad characterizing mania and the manic defense – control, contempt, and triumph – can be found in nascent form in Freud's conception of mania. The object never will be lost or missed because it is, in unconscious fantasy, under one's omnipotent control, so there is no danger of losing it; even if the object were to be lost, it would not matter because the contemptible object is "valueless" (Freud, 1917b, p. 257) and one is better off without it; moreover, being without the object is a "triumph" (p. 254), an occasion for "enjoy[ing]" (p. 257) one's emancipation from the burdensome albatross that has been hanging from one's neck.

Chapter 4

1   As will become evident, my interest in this chapter is in the inability to dream as opposed to not being able to remember one's dreams. The former involves psychotic processes while the latter usually does not.

2   Bion uses the word "thoughts" to include both thoughts and feelings.

3   For Bion (1957), there are always coexisting psychotic and non-psychotic parts of the personality. Consequently, a patient's inability to dream (which is a reflection of the psychotic part of the personality) is in every instance, to some degree accompanied by a non-psychotic part of the personality capable of alpha-function and consequently able to produce conscious thought, dream-thought, and unconscious thinking while the individual is awake.

4   Ms C had not been able to recall a single dream in the first year-and-a-half of analysis. When she began to report dreams at the end of the second year of our work, her associations to them – in the rare event that she had any at all – were very concrete, largely centering around ideas already conscious to her. My own associations to the dreams had been equally sparse and superficial and the few interpretations I made felt strained and contrived. Under other circumstances, the very fact that the patient's dreams felt dead would have constituted an important strand of meaning in its own right.

5   In other instances of reverie-deprivation in an analytic session, I have experienced great difficulty in staying awake. In the half-sleep state that has occurred under these circumstances, I have found that I dream fleeting dreams that feel similar to those that occur in sleep. At times, it seems that the function of these dreams is that of reassuring myself that I am capable of dreaming. At other times, these fleeting dreams seem to represent an unconscious effort to dream the dream that the patient is unable to dream at that point. In still other instances, my "dreams" seem to be hallucinations (often auditory) that are substitutes for dreaming intended to disguise the fact that at that moment neither the patient nor I is able to dream.

6   Only now, as I am writing this essay, am I aware of the effect of the patient's shifting tenses in recounting the dream, moving from the immediacy of the present tense ("I'm at," "It's here") in her telling the first part of the dream to the more distant, more reflective, past tense ("I looked," "There was") in telling the second part.

Chapter 5

1   Although "Mourning and melancholia" was written in 1915, Freud, for reasons that remain a mystery, chose not to publish this paper until 1917.

2   Absolute (and unknowable) Truth, referred to by Bion (1970) as O, roughly corresponds to Kant's "thing-in-itself," Plato's "Ideal Forms" and Lacan's "register of the Real." Bion, at times, labels it simply, "the experience" (1970, p. 4). In this paper, I am almost exclusively addressing humanly apprehensible, humanly meaningful, relative truths concerning human experience (as opposed to Absolute Truth).

3   My "new" thought/feeling (that R's water-soaked pants were emotionally equivalent to the urine-soaked clothing of a baby) did not necessarily represent an unearthing of a repressed aspect of my childhood experience. Rather, I conceive of the experience at the pond as having generated elements of experience (Bion's [1962a] "alpha-elements") which I stored and later "(re)-collected" in the context of what was occurring at an unconscious level in the session. My "(re)-collecting" elements of my boyhood experience was not the same as remembering that experience; in fact, it is impossible to say whether the newly re-collected aspect of the childhood experience had actually been a part of the original experience – and

it does not matter. What does matter is that elements of experience (past and present) were available to me in the form of a reverie that was true to the emotional experience that I was having with Mr V at that moment.

4   I view the co-created unconscious analytic third as standing in dialectical tension with the unconscious of the analysand and of the analyst as separate people, each with his or her own personal history, personality organization, qualities of self-consciousness, bodily experience and so on.

Chapter 6

1   This is the third in a series of papers on the subject of reading the work of major psychoanalytic writers; the first two address the experiences of reading Freud (Chapter 3) and Winnicott (Ogden, 2001c).

2   My decision to divide Bion's work into early and late periods is somewhat arbitrary. His work could, with equal validity, be divided along other lines of cleavage, for instance, by viewing *Experiences in Groups* (1959b) as a period in its own right, or by treating *Elements of Psycho-Analysis* (1963) and *Transformations* (1965) as a separate transitional period.

3   The difference between *thinking about* an experience and *being in* an experience is a recurrent theme in *Attention and Interpretation*, particularly as it relates to the impossibility of becoming an analyst by learning *about* analysis; one must be *in* psychoanalysis – one's own and the analyses one conducts – to be genuinely in the process of becoming a psychoanalyst.

4   K is a sign used by Bion (1962a) – as I interpret him – to refer not to the noun knowledge (a static body of ideas), but to knowing (or getting to know), i.e., the effort to be receptive to, and give apprehensible form (however inadequate) to what is true to an experience (O).

5   For both Bion and Borges the future is already alive in the present as "the as-yet unknown" (Bion, 1970, p. 71); the future casts its shadow backwards on the present (Bion, 1976; see also Chapter 4).

Chapter 7

1   I am reminded here of a comment made by Borges regarding proprietorship and chronology of ideas. In a preface to a volume of his poems, Borges (1964) wrote,

> If in the following pages there is some successful verse or other, may the reader forgive me the audacity of having written it before him. We are all one; our inconsequential minds are much alike, and circumstances so influence us that it is something of an accident that you are the reader and I the writer – the unsure, ardent writer – of my verses.
>
> (p. 269)

2   I am indebted to Dr Margaret Fulton for drawing my attention to Poe's poem.

Chapter 8

1   I use the terms *voice* and *tone* to refer to different aspects of speaking/writing. Tone reflects what the speaker is feeling; voice reflects who the speaker is, the way he thinks, how he organizes his emotional experience. Of course, the two overlap.

2   I am reminded here of what the doctor in Berger's (1967) *A Fortunate Man* said of common sense: "When dealing with human beings it is my biggest enemy . . . it tempts me to accept the obvious, the easiest, the most readily available answer" (p. 62).

Bibliography

Balint, M. (1968). *The Basic Fault*. London: Tavistock.

Berger, J. (1967). *A Fortunate Man*. New York: Pantheon.

Bion, W. R. (1957). Differentiation of the psychotic from the non-psychotic personalities. In *Second Thoughts* (pp. 43–64). New York: Aronson, 1967.

Bion, W. R. (1959a). Attacks on linking. In *Second Thoughts* (pp. 93–109). New York: Aronson, 1967.

Bion, W. R. (1959b). *Experiences in Groups*. London: Tavistock.

Bion, W. R. (1959c). 27 July 1959. In *Cogitations* (p. 43). London: Karnac, 1992.

Bion, W. R. (1962a). *Learning from experience*. In *Seven Servants*. New York: Aronson, 1977.

Bion, W. R. (1962b). A theory of thinking. In *Second Thoughts* (pp. 110–119). New York: Aronson, 1967.

Bion, W. R. (1963). *Elements of psycho-Analysis*. In *Seven Servants*. New York: Aronson, 1977.

Bion, W. R. (1965). *Transformations*. In *Seven Servants*. New York: Aronson, 1977.

Bion, W. R. (1967). *Second Thoughts*. New York: Aronson.

Bion, W. R. (1970). *Attention and interpretation*. In *Seven Servants*. New York: Aronson, 1977.

Bion, W. R. (1975). Brasilia clinical seminars. In *Clinical Seminars and Four Papers* (pp. 1–118). Abingdon, England: Fleetwood Press, 1987.

Bion, W. R. (1976). On a quotation from Freud. In *Clinical Seminars and Four Papers* (pp. 234–238). Abingdon, England: Fleetwood Press, 1987.

Bion, W. R. (1978). Sao Paulo clinical seminars. In *Clinical Seminars and Four Papers* (pp. 131–220). Abingdon, England: Fleetwood Press, 1987.

Bion, W. R. (1982). *The Long Week-End, 1897–1919*. Abingdon, England: Fleetwood Press.

Bion, W. R. (1992). *Cogitations* (F. Bion, ed.). London: Karnac.

Borges, J. L. (1923). Preface to the 1923 edition of *Fervor de Buenos Aires*. In N. T. Di Giovanni (ed.), *Jorge Luis Borges: Selected Poems, 1923–1967* (pp. 268–269). New York: Dell, 1972.

Borges, J. L. (1941a). Funes the memorious. In J. Irby (trans.) and D. Yates and J. Irby (eds), *Labyrinths: Selected Stories and Other Writings* (pp. 59–66). New York: New Directions, 1962.

Borges, J. L. (1941b). Pierre Menard, author of the *Quixote*. In J. Irby (trans.) and D. Yates and J. Irby (eds), *Labyrinths: Selected Stories and Other Writings* (pp. 36–44). New York: New Directions, 1962.

Borges, J. L. (1946). A new refutation of time. In J. Irby (trans.) and D. Yates and J. Irby (eds), *Labyrinths: Selected Stories and Other Writings* (pp. 217–234). New York: New Directions, 1962.

Borges, J. L. (1949). Everything and nothing. In J. Irby (trans.) and D. Yates and J. Irby (eds), *Labyrinths: Selected Stories and Other Writings* (pp. 248–249). New York: New Directions, 1962.

Borges, J. L. (1957). Borges and I. In J. Irby (trans.) and D. Yates and J. Irby (eds), *Labyrinths: Selected Stories and Other Writings* (pp. 246–247). New York: New Directions, 1962.

Borges, J. L. (1964). Foreword. In N. T. Di Giovanni (ed. and trans.), *Jorge Luis Borges: Selected Poems, 1923–1967* (p. 272). New York: Dell, 1972.

Borges, J. L . (1967). *This Craft of Verse* (C.-A. Mihăilescu, ed.). Cambridge, MA: Harvard University Press, 2000.

Borges, J. L. (1970a). An autobiographical essay. In N. T. Di Giovanni in collaboration with J. L. Borges (ed. and trans.), *The Aleph and Other Stories, 1939–1969* (pp. 203–260). New York: Dutton, 1970.

Borges, J. L. (1970b). Preface. In N. T. Di Giovanni (trans.), *Doctor Brodie's Report* (pp. 11–14). London: Penguin, 1976.

Borges, J. L. (1975). Interview in *La Nación*, November 24, 1974. In E. Williamson (trans.), *Borges: A Life* (p. 412). New York: Viking, 2004.

Borges, J. L. (1984). *Twenty-four Conversations with Borges: Interviews with Roberto Alifano, 1981–1983* (including a selection of poems) (trans. N. S. Araúz, W. Barnstone and N. Escandell). Housatonic, MA: Lascaux.

Cambray, J. (2002). Synchronicity and emergence. *American Imago* 59: 409–434.

Daws, D. (1989). *Through the Night: Helping Parents and Sleepless Infants*. London: Free Association Books.

de M'Uzan, M. (1984). Slaves of quantity. *Psychoanalytic Quarterly*, 72: 711–725, 2003.

Fairbairn, W. R. D. (1944). Endopsychic structure considered in terms of object-relationships. In *Psychoanalytic Studies of the Personality* (pp. 82–136). London: Routledge and Kegan Paul, 1981.

Fairbairn, W. R. D. (1952). *Psychoanalytic Studies of the Personality*. London: Routledge and Kegan Paul, 1981.

Freud, S. (1900). *The Interpretation of Dreams*. SE 4–5. (*The Standard Edition of the Complete Psychological Works of Sigmund Freud*. J. Strachey (ed. and trans.), London: Hogarth Press, 1974.)

Freud, S. (1911–1915). Papers on technique. SE 12.

Freud, S. (1914a). On the history of the psycho-analytic movement. SE 14.

Freud, S. (1914b). On narcissism: an introduction. SE 14.

Freud, S. (1915a). Instincts and their vicissitudes. SE 14.

Freud, S. (1915b). Repression. SE 14.

Freud, S. (1915c). The unconscious. SE 14.

Freud, S. (1916–17). *Introductory Lectures on Psycho-Analysis*. SE 16.

Freud, S. (1917a). A metapsychological supplement to the theory of dreams. SE 14.

Freud, S. (1917b). Mourning and melancholia. SE 14.

Freud, S. (1918). From the history of an infantile neurosis. SE 17.

Freud, S. (1923). Two encyclopaedia articles. SE 18.

Freud, S. (1933). *New Introductory Lectures*. SE 22.

Frost, R. (1928). Acquainted with the night. In R. Poirier and M. Richardson (eds), *Robert Frost: Collected Poems, Prose and Plays* (p. 234). New York: Library of America, 1995.

Frost, R. (1930). Education by poetry. In R. Poirier and M. Richardson (eds), *Robert Frost: Collected Poems, Prose and Plays* (pp. 717–728). New York, Library of America, 1995.

Frost, R. (1939). The figure a poem makes. In R. Poirier and M. Richardson (eds), *Robert Frost: Collected Poems, Prose and Plays* (pp.776–778). New York: Library of America, 1995.

Frost, R. (1942a). Carpe diem. In R. Poirier and M. Richardson (eds), *Robert Frost: Collected Poems, Prose and Plays* (p. 305). New York: Library of America, 1995.

Frost, R. (1942b). I could give all to time. In R. Poirier and M. Richardson (eds), *Robert Frost: Collected Poems, Prose and Plays* (pp. 304–305). New York: Library of America, 1995.

Gay, P. (1988). *Freud: A Life For Our Time*. New York: Norton.

Goethe, J. W. (1808). *Faust I and II*. In S. Atkins (ed. and trans.), *Goethe: The Collected Works* (Vol. 2). Princeton NJ: Princeton University Press, 1984.

Green, A. (1983). The dead mother. In *Private Madness* (pp. 142–173). Madison, CT: International Universities Press, 1980.

Hartmann, E. (1984). *The Nightmare*. New York: Basic Books.

Heaney, S. (1979). Song. In *Opened Ground: Selected Poems, 1966–1996* (p.173). New York: Farrar, Straus and Giroux, 1998.

Heaney, S. (1984). Clearances. In *Opened Ground: Selected Poems, 1966–1996* (pp. 282–290). New York: Farrar, Straus and Giroux, 1998.

Jarrell, R. (1955). To the Laodiceans. In *Poetry and the Age* (pp. 34–62). New York: Vintage.

Joseph, B. (1985). Transference: the total situation. *International Journal of Psychoanalysis*, 66: 447–454.

Klein, M. (1935). A contribution to the psychogenesis of manic-depressive states. In *Contributions to Psycho-Analysis, 1921–1945* (pp. 282–310). London: Hogarth Press, 1968.

Klein, M. (1940). Mourning and its relations to manic-depressive states. In *Contributions to Psycho-Analysis, 1921–1945* (pp. 311–338). London: Hogarth Press, 1968.

Klein, M. (1952). Some theoretical conclusions regarding the emotional life of the infant. In *Envy and Gratitude and Other Works, 1946–1963* (pp. 61–93). New York: Delacorte, 1975.

Leonard, E. (1991). *The Writer's Quotation Book* (p. 32). (J. Charlton, ed.). New York: Penguin.

Loewald, H. (1960). On the therapeutic action of psychoanalysis. In *Papers on Psychoanalysis* (pp. 221–256). New Haven, CT: Yale University Press, 1980.

Loewald, H. (1978). Primary process, secondary process and language. In *Papers on Psychoanalysis* (pp. 178–206). New Haven, CT: Yale University Press, 1980.

McDougall, J. (1984). The "dis-affected" patient: reflections on affect pathology. *Psychoanalytic Quarterly*, 53: 386–409.

McLaughlin, B.P. (1992). The rise and fall of British emergentism. In A. Beckermann, H. Flohr, and J. Kim (eds), *Emergence or Reduction? Essays on the Prospects of Non-reductive Physicalism*. Berlin, NY: Walter de Gruyter.

Mandelstam, O. (1933). Conversation about Dante. In J. Harris (ed.) and J Harris and C Link (trans.), *Osip Mandelstam: The Complete Critical Prose* (pp. 252–290). Dana Point, CA: Ardis, 1997.

Ogden, T. (1980). On the nature of schizophrenic conflict. *International Journal of Psychoanalysis*, 61: 513–533.

Ogden, T. (1982). *Projective Identification and Psychotherapeutic Technique*. Northvale, NJ: Aronson/London: Karnac.

Ogden, T. (1983). The concept of internal object relations. *International Journal of Psychoanalysis*, 64: 227–241.

Ogden, T. (1989). The initial analytic meeting. In *The Primitive Edge of Experience* (pp. 169–194). Northvale, NJ: Aronson/London: Karnac.

Ogden, T. (1994a). The analytic third: working with intersubjective clinical facts. *International Journal of Psychoanalysis*, 75: 3–20.

Ogden, T. (1994b). The concept of interpretive action. *Psychoanalytic Quarterly*, 63: 219–245.

Ogden, T. (1994c). *Subjects of Analysis*. Northvale, NJ: Aronson/London: Karnac.

Ogden, T. (1995). Analysing forms of aliveness and deadness of the transference–countertransference. *International Journal of Psychoanalysis*, 76: 695–709.

Ogden, T. (1996). Reconsidering three aspects of psychoanalytic technique. *International Journal of Psychoanalysis*, 77: 883–899.

Ogden, T. (1997a). Reverie and interpretation. *Psychoanalytic Quarterly* 66: 567–595.

Ogden, T. (1997b). *Reverie and Interpretation: Sensing Something Human*. Northvale, NJ: Aronson/London: Karnac.

Ogden, T. (1997c). Reverie and metaphor: Some thoughts on how I work as a psychoanalyst. *International Journal of Psychoanalysis*, 78: 719–732.

Ogden, T. (1999a). The analytic third: an overview. In L. Aron and S. Mitchell (eds), *Relational Psychoanalysis: The Emergence of a Tradition* (pp. 487–492). Hillsdale, NJ: Analytic Press.

Ogden, T. (1999b). 'The music of what happens' in poetry and psychoanalysis. *International Journal of Psychoanalysis*, 80: 979–994.

Ogden, T. (2001a). *Conversations at the Frontier of Dreaming*. Northvale, NJ: Aronson/London: Karnac.

Ogden, T. (2001b). Conversations at the frontier of dreaming. In *Conversations at the Frontier of Dreaming* (pp. 1–14). Northvale, NJ: Aronson/London: Karnac.

Ogden, T. (2001c). Reading Winnicott. *Psychoanalytic Quarterly*, 70: 299–323.

Ogden, T. (2002). A new reading of the origins of object-relations theory. *International Journal of Psychoanalysis*, 83:767–782.

Ogden, T. (2003a). On not being able to dream. *International Journal of Psychoanalysis*, 84: 17–30.

Ogden, T. (2003b). What's true and whose idea was it? *International Journal of Psychoanalysis*, 84: 593–606.

Ogden, T. (2004a). An introduction to the reading of Bion. *International Journal of Psychoanalysis*, 85: 285–300.

Ogden, T (2004b). This art of psychoanalysis: Dreaming undreamt dreams and interrupted cries. *International Journal of Psychoanalysis*, 85: 857–877.

Pinsky, R. (1988). *Poetry and the World*. New York: Ecco.

Poe, E.A. (1848). To _____ _____ _____. In *The Complete Tales and Poems of Edgar Allan Poe* (p. 80). New York: Barnes and Noble, 1992.

Pritchard, W. (1991). Ear training. In *Teaching What We Do* (pp. 127–144). Amherst, MA: Amherst College Press, 1991.

Rosenfeld, D. (2004). September 11th : Military dictatorship and psychotic episode. Unpublished manuscript.

Searles H. (1975). The patient as therapist to his analyst. In *Countertransference and Related Subjects* (pp. 380–459). New York: International Universities Press, 1979.

Stoppard, T. (1999). Pragmatic theater. *The New York Review of Books*, XLVI, no. 14, Sept. 23, 1999, pp. 8–10.

Strachey, J. (1957). Papers on metapsychology: Editor's introduction. SE 14, 105–107.

Tresan, D. (1996). Jungian metapsychology and neurobiological theory. *Journal of Analytical Psychology*, 41: 399–436.

Trilling, L. (1947). Freud and literature. In *The Liberal Imagination* (pp. 32–54). New York: Anchor, 1953.

Tustin F. (1981). *Autistic States in Children*. Boston: Routledge and Kegan Paul.

Varnum, R. (1996). *Fencing with Words: A History of Writing Instruction at Amherst College During the Years of Theodore Baird, 1938–1966*. Urbana, IL: National Council of Teachers of English.

Vendler, H. (1997). *Poems, Poets, Poetry*. Boston: Bedford Books.

Weinstein, A. (1998). Audio tape lecture 1. In *Classics of American Literature*. Chantilly, VA: Teaching Company.

Williams, W. C. (1932). Letter to Kay Boyle. In J. Thirlwall (ed.), *The Selected Letters of William Carlos Williams* (p. 129). New York: New Directions, 1984.

Winnicott, D. W. (1945). Primitive emotional development. In *Through Paediatrics to Psycho-Analysis* (pp. 145–156). New York: Basic Books, 1975.

Winnicott, D. W. (1949). Mind and its relation to the psyche-soma. In *Through Paediatrics to Psycho-Analysis* (pp. 243–254). New York: Basic Books, 1975.

Winnicott, D. W. (1951). Transitional objects and transitional phenomena. In *Through Paediatrics to Psycho-Analysis* (pp. 229–242). New York: Basic Books, 1975.

Winnicott, D. W. (1954a). The depressive position in normal emotional development. In *Through Paediatrics to Psycho-Analysis* (pp. 262–277). New York: Basic Books, 1975.

Winnicott, D. W. (1954b). Metapsychological and clinical aspects of regression within the 'psycho-analytical set-up.' In *Through Paediatrics to Psycho-Analysis* (pp. 278–294). New York: Basic Books, 1975.

Winnicott, D. W. (1955). Group influences and the maladjusted child: the school aspect. In *The Family and Individual Development* (pp. 146–155). London: Tavistock, 1965.

Winnicott, D. W. (1956). Primary maternal preoccupation. In *Through Paediatrics to Psycho-Analysis* (pp. 300–305). New York: Basic Books, 1975.

Winnicott, D. W. (1958). The capacity to be alone. In *The Maturational Processes and the*

Facilitating Environment (pp. 29–36). New York: International Universities Press, 1965.

Winnicott, D. W. (1962). The aims of psycho-analytical treatment. In *The Maturational Processes and the Facilitating Environment* (pp. 166–170). New York: International Universities Press, 1965.

Winnicott, D. W. (1964). *The Child, the Family, and the Outside World*. Baltimore, MD: Pelican.

Winnicott, D. W. (1971a). The place where we live. In *Playing and Reality* (pp. 104–110). New York: Basic Books.

Winnicott, D. W. (1971b). Transitional objects and transitional phenomena. In *Playing and Reality* (pp. 1–25). New York: Basic Books.

Winnicott, D. W. (1974). Fear of breakdown. *International Review of Psychoanalysis*, 1: 103–107.

Wood, M. (1994). *The Magician's Doubts: Nabokov and the Risks of Fiction*. Princeton, NJ: Princeton University Press.

Index